In memory of
Spyros Panagiotis Skouras
(1893-1971)

The
Cleopatra
Files

Selected Documents from the
Spyros P. Skouras Archive

Edited by
Ilias Chrissochoidis

Brave World
Stanford, 2013

Contents

Introduction
Cleopatra at Fifty

Twentieth Century Fox's *Cleopatra* (1963) was more than a milestone in Hollywood extravagance. As the most costly and "mis-produced" film to date, it marked a permanent rift between talent and management in an iconic American industry. Under the old studio system, stars like Elizabeth Taylor were nothing but employees whose image and even life were shaped by the company's publicity staff. Massive loss of revenue in the postwar years brought most studios to their knees and helped loosen their control over creative talent. *Cleopatra* would become the first instance where artists nearly destroyed a studio.

For fifty years now the runaway production has been described from the perspective of "disillusioned" insiders. Even before the release of the film, producer Walter Wanger, director Joseph L. Mankiewicz and the Taylor-Burton couple lashed against Twentieth Century-Fox for allegedly interfering with a cinematic masterpiece. Their comments were especially harmful to its President Spyros P. Skouras who after leading the company for twenty years assumed everyone else's responsibility and resigned. Unlike his accusers, he never went public with his version of the story. Instead, he kept the production's files in his archive, which now are part of the "Spyros P. Skouras Papers" at Stanford University.

The "Cleopatra files" reveal extensive abuse of Skouras's trust and the company's financial resources by the film's creative team. It was a strategic mistake for the studio to entrust a big production to freelancers instead of using its own contracted talent. Walter Wanger, an independent producer for the previous twenty years, repeatedly breached the company's

protocol and started approaching agents and lawyers behind
Fox's back, thus compromising the company's negotiating
position. His obsession with Elizabeth Taylor as Cleopatra cost
millions to Fox and proved nearly fatal for both the actress and
the production. Worst of all, he failed to perform his executive
responsibilities during the mammoth shooting in Rome, the
main reason for the studio's financial hemorrhage. Instead of
accepting his share of blame, Wanger whitewashed himself,
Mankiewicz and Taylor with a morally spurious and factually
contestable diary.

By the time she was hired to portray Cleopatra, Taylor
had been chronically dependent on sleeping pills and painkill-
ers, making her vulnerable to infections. Aside from her
preposterous financial demands (which included lucrative post-
Cleopatra deals), she also dictated the move of the production
overseas and the choice of Mankiewicz as its director. No
actress before and seldom afterwards has been so generously
treated by a studio, while repeatedly breaching her contract.
During the epic 228-day shooting in Rome, Taylor worked only
122 days, 99 of which she was late, often leading to cancelled
sessions. To top everything, her affair with Richard Burton
caused worldwide furor, put enormous pressure on Fox, a
publicly owned company of 35,000 stockholders, and not least
destroyed two families. Taylor's hypocritical loathing of the
film that made her a multimillionaire and a world icon indicates
the rift between Hollywood talent and management in the early
1960s.

The chief responsibility for the financial chaos of
Cleopatra falls on the shoulders of its creator, Joseph L.
Mankiewicz. Hired on the most lucrative terms offered to a
director by then and enjoying unprecedented creative freedom,
Mankiewicz indulged his artistic ambitions to a degree that
derailed the production's budget. His demand to shoot *Cleopatra* in Rome deprived Fox from checking his actions and

expenses. Although a new script was ready by August, he determined to improve it while shooting the movie. His double duties as writer and director led to physical and mental exhaustion. Failing to meet one deadline after another, he wrapped up production on July 28, 1963, seven months later than Fox expected. His decision to shoot in continuity cost the production seven-and-a-half million dollars alone, and the thousands that were kept on payroll for 230 days at a daily cost of $125,000 almost ruined Twentieth Century-Fox. Returning to America, he stubbornly refused to cut the film below four hours and when incoming Fox President Darryl F. Zanuck exercised his authority to salvage the film, Mankiewicz went to the press accusing the company of stealing his film.

The combined effect of Mankiewicz's extravagant filmmaking, Wanger's executive incompetence, and Taylor's unprofessional attitude sunk the film's budget by an extra 20 million dollars. Remarkably, the same people that were emptying the coffers of Twentieth Century-Fox, presented themselves as martyrs of corporate abuse. The mixed legacy of *Cleopatra* fifty years later is a reminder that, while art and business should not be onscreen bedfellows, they should be kept vigilant of each other's dark side in all other occasions.

The present volume makes available to the public key documents on the production of *Cleopatra*. It is the fruit of a year-long research on Spyros P. Skouras' life and achievements conducted at Stanford University. I am grateful to the Stanford Library Department of Special Collections for facilitating my research as well as to Skouras' son Spyros Solon and relatives both in the US and in Europe for endorsing my work. Along with my Stanford research portal and compilation of Skouras' memoirs, this volume is dedicated to the 120th birth anniversary of the most influential Greek immigrant in American history.

Ilias Chrissochoidis

Profiles

Adler, Buddy: Head of Production from 1956 until his death in 1960.

Brown, David: Head of the story department since 1951.

Goldstein, Robert: successor of Adler as Head of the Studio.

Koegel, Otto: lawyer and Twentieth Century-Fox's chief counsel.

Levathes, Peter G.: Head of Studio from 1961 to 1962.

Mamoulian, Rouben: Director of the London-based production of *Cleopatra*.

Mankiewicz, Joseph L.: Director and writer of the Rome-based production of *Cleopatra*.

Merman, Doc: Twentieth Century-Fox's production manager.

Nizer, Louis: legendary trial lawyer and personal friend of Skouras.

Rogell, Sidney: production manager of the Rome-based *Cleopatra*.

Skouras, Spyros P.: President (1942–62) and Chairman of the Board (1962–69) of Twentieth Century-Fox Film Corporation.

Wanger, Walter: Producer of *Cleopatra*.

Zanuck, Darryl F.: Co-founder, Head of Studio until 1956, and Skouras' successor in the presidency of Twentieth Century-Fox Film Corporation (1962–).

The *Cleopatra* Files

Skouras' account of *Cleopatra* (1962)

The following letter, addressed to Darryl F. Zanuck, was drafted on May 31, 1962, one month before Skouras resigned as President of Twentieth Century-Fox. It was slightly re-worked on September 27 and typed in official stationery on October 8. It was never sent, presumably because of the rift between Zanuck and Joe Mankiewicz on account of the editing of Cleopatra.

> Dear Darryl:
>
> I have read Joe Mankiewicz' letter to you regarding "CLEOPATRA" and, naturally, I am very much relieved and happy that he is so enthusiastic about the great possibilities of this picture. Of course I personally expect it to be the greatest boxoffice attraction of all time.
>
> For your information however – and if you so desire you can show this letter to Joe when you see him – I would like to give you the facts surrounding the production of this picture.
>
> At the outset let me say that as President of the Corporation during this production, I assume all the responsibility and am not trying to blame others for the mistakes which occurred, but rather to set the facts straight.
>
> As you know, we engaged Joe in February 1961 to succeed Rouben Mamoulian. We bought out his company – Figaro Productions Inc. – and thereby placed him in a very good financial position. This was an extremely good deal for Joe who expressed his ap-

preciation many times because he felt he gained for himself the security he desired.

Joe stepped into the picture immediately and worked very hard, doing his utmost to improve the script we had at the time. He engaged various writers, among them Sidney Buchman, to help with the rewrites.

Unfortunately, shortly after Joe's arrival in London, Elizabeth Taylor had a relapse, and became violently ill – which almost proved fatal for her. After her recovery, the decision was made to abandon all production activities in London and make the picture in Los Angeles.

I must emphasize that his contract gave him wide discretion and authority. In addition, I gave him a free hand in engaging anyone he wanted to enable him to produce a great picture. And, I might add that from the beginning I did my utmost to encourage him in every way possible to make an outstanding production.

As you know, up to this time Joe was not considered to be an extravagant director, or an extravagant producer-director when he became an independent producer.

Immediately after the London production was abandoned, he decided to set aside the old script completely and engaged Randy McDougall to write a new one.

As soon as he returned to Los Angeles, he started a campaign to have the picture made in Italy. I became alarmed because of the bitter experience we had in London and I did not want to venture into any production with Elizabeth Taylor overseas. I was just as apprehensive about the consequences of making the picture in Italy with Elizabeth as I was when the production was to be made in Great Britain.

I had many arguments with Buddy Adler who, for some reason, desired that CLEOPATRA be made in Europe because he felt that we could have another "BEN HUR."

Joe favored moving the production to Italy because he felt the climate, sea and atmosphere was much better than in Los Angeles; he claimed he was thoroughly familiar with the production facilities at Cinecitta – which were equally as good as ours; that the picture could be made more economically not only because of the favorable rates for Italian labor and the six-day week, but the people there worked harder. Also, he felt the greatness of the picture would be more effective if it were made in Italy.

As soon as Taylor recovered in the late spring of 1961, Martin Gang and Kurt Fring met with Peter Levathes, Frank Ferguson and Doc Merman. They stated that the Taylor contract would have to be renegotiated in order to offset the benefits she would have received if the picture was to be made in the United States instead of overseas because Taylor had the legal right to have the picture produced in Europe.

When Joe Mankiewicz heard this, he then went all-out to convince everyone that the picture should be made in Italy. He stated that this was his preference above everything and repeated the facilities that were available at Cinecitta. Walter Wanger joined Joe in pressing for the removal of the production in Europe even though we had already begun set construction in Hollywood.

I personally was strongly opposed to this, because I was afraid that we would meet insurmountable difficulties, particularly in view of Elizabeth's health and fear of what her behavior would be if she were away from the studio, but they were successful in convincing the studio that CLEOPATRA should be produced in Italy.

Eddie Fisher and Dr. Rex Kennamer, Elizabeth's personal physician, concurred with me that the picture should be made in Los Angeles.

But then there were many conferences, talks and negotiations with Peter Levathes and his staff, and Joe was successful in convincing the studio that large sums of money could be saved if the production was made in Italy.

During this period, Dr. Kennamer happened to be in New York attending some medical convention. Joe phoned me and asked that I contact Dr. Kennamer in order to obtain his approval for making the picture in Italy. Dr. Kennamer came to see me – Otto Koegel and Joe Moskowitz were with me. We phoned Los Angeles and talked to Levathes and Mankiewicz, as well as to Eddie Fisher, Martin Gang and Kurt Fring. Then Dr. Kennamer said he would think the matter over.

The following day, Dr. Kennamer again came to see me, but this time his mind was completely changed. He felt it would be alright to move the production to Rome if he would be able to accompany Elizabeth and stay with her until she was sufficiently advanced in the production. He stated that this time it made no difference whether the picture would be made in Los Angeles or Rome – the risk would be the same. But by being with her, he would see that she had every attention and prevent her from catching colds.

Kurt Fring and Martin Gang went to see Levathes and Ferguson to advise them that based upon

Taylor's original contract she wanted to make the picture in Europe. Levathes communicated this message to me and Otto advised me that she had that right. I then told the studio to negotiate and see what they could do about it.

However, Elizabeth demanded that she be given the right to make the picture in Italy. We then consented with the assurance that Dr. Kennamer would accompany her, although I was reluctant and greatly worried: (a) because of her health, and (b) while our studio would be idle, we would have to pay out-of-pocket money to rent Cinecitta – and we would have the same experience as we had in London. But in view of the opinion expressed by our counsel, I could not oppose this decision.

When this was settled, Fring and Gang met with Levathes and stated that Taylor was now ready to go back to work and that she would have to report at the latest by September or else she would have to either cancel from appearing in CLEOPATRA or be given the right to appear in another picture.

At a meeting with Levathes, Doc Merman, Wanger and Johnson, Joe told them that a mid-September date could be met. I advised Levathes not to set a starting date but to wait until Mankiewicz and Wanger agreed upon a definite date, and he informed me later that Joe and Walter set September 17th as the starting date of this production, which date was inserted in Taylor's contract.

The first time I met with Joe in Rome, as well as up to this time, he has taken the position that this date was handed to him in an arbitrary manner, whereas the truth is that he, Walter – as well as his Unit Manager, Johnny Johnson – were informed at all times of

the negotiations that were going on with Taylor and
they acceded to this date, assuring the studio that it was
a realistic date that could be met. Joe left for Italy in July 1961 to make the necessary preparation for the production.

By August, Randy McDougall had written the
script – and I have been told by everyone that this was
the basic script. There is no question that Joe did a
great job in taking the McDougall script and moderniz-
ing the dialogue and bringing the story down to earth.
When you see the picture I am sure you will be tre-
mendously impressed by what Joe did.

It is my opinion that although the story is based
on the stories of Plutarch, Shakespeare and Bernard
Shaw, his conception of the story, as well as the dialogue, surpasses any man's greatest expectations – and I
say this from the scenes I have seen.

With regard to the many announcements in the
press by Joe that he was shooting from page to page,
this is not true because when Peter and I went   to
Rome in November, 1961 (because of our concern regarding the budget) at a meeting at the Grand Hotel
with all the heads of the departments (about 20 persons) someone complained to Joe that we did not have
a script and he stated that they could be guided by the
McDougall script and make the sets accordingly since
he was making changes only in the dialogue; that he
might add some scenes in which case they would be
notified.

The only difference between the McDougall
script and the final shooting script was a sharpening up
of the dialogue. Joe added some scenes and elaborated
on some of the scenes in the McDougall script. Therefore his statement to the press from time to time that

he was shooting from page to page was unfairly exaggerated.

As I have stated previously, Joe insisted upon a free hand in the selection of his own production unit. [May 31 draft: Joe had a free hand in setting up the CLEOPATRA unit. Everything regarding the preparation of this production was under his personal control; he demanded complete autonomy as to every move. He insisted that Walter Wanger be the producer and that he needed him.] He personally picked Johnny Johnson and clothed him with full authority to make all arrangements in Italy. [May 31 draft: Joe chose as unit manager Johnny Johnson, for whom the job was too big and who, although I am sure he was not aware of this, was a very sick man and had to have blood transfusions while working and finally passed away, as you know, several months after the beginning of the picture.] Under Joe's supervision, Johnson together with John DeCuir (the production designer) made commitments for the stages, contracts for leasing of locations, so that by the end of August 1961, the sets and costumes were well under way.

When we decided to make the picture in Italy, Joe engaged Franco Magli, whom he designated as the Italian Unit Manager, and all negotiations and contracts with Cinecitta and Italian suppliers were undertaken under his supervision.

[May 31 draft: unfortunately, Magli proved to be completely untrustworthy.] In September the studio raised the question of Magli's trustworthiness and Joe stated that he would vouch for his honesty. He objected to his replacement and in deference to him Magli was retained.

Joe had requested – and Walter with Doc Merman followed through – in sending between 80 to 90 studio people to Italy by the end of August and early September. This large number of Hollywood personnel in Rome greatly alarmed everyone at the studio and Levathes telephoned me that we should send someone there to supervise the expenditures for this operation. He suggested Sid Rogell.

I phoned Joe and told him that we were arranging to send Rogell; he told me that he had no objection and felt the studio should have some representative in Rome to properly watch the expenses. Consequently, I took Rogell to Rome with me on September 2, 1961. [September 27 draft: when I went there with Sid, although he did not object to him, he did not like the idea as he preferred Johnny Johnson. He did agree, however, that no money should be spent without Rogell's approval.]

We spent several days going over the commitments that had been made up to that time and got into a thorough discussion on the budget that lasted for several days. The heads of the departments were requested by Joe to make up the expenditures they would need for the production and they presented me with a budget totaling $14,057,992.22. Joe took the position that it would be utterly ridiculous for this picture to cost $14,000,000 and requested each department to adjust their figures.

We held a two-day meeting, and I participated with every department head. They made suggestions as to what should be spent and presented it to Joe. He approved their suggestions. They succeeded in reducing their figure for sets, costumes, extras and many other items and brought the budget down to $10,413,872.60

and Joe instructed each department head to keep within this budget. He further stated that if there would be
any change in this figure they would advise us in New
York.

This figure was presented to the Board upon
my return on September 22, 1961.

However, during the first week in November –
much to our surprise – the budget of $10,413,872 was
not adhered to, instead the costs kept mounting. The
studio and our New York accountants advised us that
the figure looked more like $20,000,000.

Naturally, we became greatly alarmed and then
on November 15, 1961, Levathes and I went to Rome
to correct the situation. We had long meetings with
every department head and general meetings with Walter and Joe which lasted more than a week.

In the presence of all the department heads –
on a Sunday afternoon in the Grand Hotel – Joe stated
the $20,000,000 figure was ridiculous, but insisted that
if he had a realistic amount and someone would tell
him how much had been actually spent up to that
point, then he felt with an additional $5,000,000 the
picture could be completed. (Johnson was still there at
this time.)

During the Christmas holidays, Wanger arrived
in New York and advised us that the budget now
looked like $20,000,000 and in a conference with
Michel, Koegel, Levathes and Moskowitz, I protested
strenuously because I could not understand how the
budget was increased without their notifying us.

Wanger blamed New York for $5,000,000 of
the cost and claimed that all the trouble was caused because he did not have proper authority as the producer

and blamed me for giving Joe full authority. I then asked what was he and Sid Rogell doing in Rome.

He stated that New York had insisted on starting the picture ahead of time, but I told him that this was not true because New York had nothing to do with the starting date of the picture. This entire matter was decided by the studio, between Levathes, Walter and Joe. I remarked that this was a familiar complaint of Walter's and that he did have the authority as the producer because he was receiving a large salary and expenses and he also had an interest in the picture.

Many times he was requested to talk to Joe, but each time Wanger said he did not want to oppose Joe's wishes. He acted more like an observer than the producer of the picture.

The record will show that both he and Joe were given everything they required to make a great picture and to complete the production as soon as possible. Joe promised that he would get through with Elizabeth as fast as possible and that he hoped to get her scenes through by February, but not later than March.

We furnished them with the most capable stars, the heads of every department from our studio – who were stationed in Italy practically throughout the entire production, as well as prop makers, craftsmen and technicians of all kinds.

Without approval or consultation, Joe and Walter made commitments of great magnitude and we were confronted with these commitments later. An example of this is the decision to build a fleet of life-size warships at fantastic costs that have not been fully audited yet. We spent several hundreds of thousands of dollars building a process lake on the ranch for the purpose of doing the battle scenes there. Both Joe and

Walter were aware of this because it was done at their request. Yet they proceeded to spend well over a million dollars for the construction of an Egyptian and Roman fleet for the Tarsus and Battle of Actium scenes.

Time and again we asked Joe to make his cuts on the script, but he insisted "he did not have time to revise the script but would have to cut it after it was shot." [September 27 draft: in his polishing of the MacDougall script, he expanded it to almost 400 pages so that millions of dollars went into sequences that are going to wind up on the cutting room floor.] Perhaps the greatest area of waste in the film is the excessive footage that was shot by Joe. I am sure you have seen the logs of the production department where he has exceeded 600,000 feet of negative, which is something of a record in the history of the business.

Even as late as May 1962, there seemed to be no indication that this picture was coming to an end. Joe talked of elaborate sequences in Ischia, big confrontations of troops in Egypt, and we became so alarmed that Koegel, Moskowitz and Levathes went to Rome on May 31st armed with a formal resolution of the Executive Committee setting definite end dates so that this picture could finally wind up. Even this committee – representing various departments of the company – found their difficulties with Joe who insisted on a free hand to continue to shoot endless footage.

I am not writing this to criticize Joe but since you permitted me to share his letter to you, I must set the record straight.

At no time was there a hint that the cost would reach the exorbitant figure it has now reached. I had insisted that the studio evolve some budget as early as

May 1961. At that time, we were talking about a $10,000,000 budget. You can readily see from the enclosed copy of a wire I received on May 19, 1961, the results of a meeting Bob Goldstein had with Joe, Walter and Johnson, where they informed New York that the figure of $8,000,000 to $10,000,000 was the nearest they could come to the budget. Even as an approximate cost it is a long way from the final cost of the picture.

Five days later, as the attached May 24th teletype will show, they attempted to further refine the figure, indicating that they arrived at it with a sense of responsibility and seriousness, also showing what kind of money Joe had in mind to spend on this production and that it was never the intention to go as far afield as he went.

When I heard that almost 100 persons had been transferred from the studio to Italy at the request of Joe through Johnson, I became greatly alarmed. We were practically transferring our entire studio to Italy, and when I informed Joe last winter that the cost would surpass the $10,000,000 mark, he was astounded.

Neither Walter nor Joe can say that they did not have full authority. Walter complains that the authority had been given to Joe, but Joe and Walter worked hand in hand. Joe participated in all three meetings which we held with all the department heads in Rome and was shocked at the amount of money being spent. He disclaims responsibility for the sets, but John DeCuir and those responsible for making the sets told us that Joe approved every design and every sketch. He not only approved every set but all the locations, including Anzio which he personally scouted from a motorboat and personally selected.

Anything regarding the preparation and administration of this production was under Joe's personal control; he demanded complete autonomy and, although he claims that he was never informed about the various elements connected with the making of this picture, he not only had complete knowledge but full control of where the production was going.

Let me repeat, that this letter is not being sent in criticism of anyone connected with the production, but simply to set the record straight.

Affectionate regards.

Sincerely,

Preproduction (1958–60)

1956–58

[Brown to Adler, April 25, 1960]

Dear Buddy:

The history of CLEOPATRA in this company goes back to 1917 when we made the film with Theda Bara but the recent history of the project, as it pertains to Walter Wanger, is this.

On April 23, 1956, I wrote a memorandum to James Mason and Arthur Kramer stating that I liked the idea of doing a film on CLEOPATRA and asking if Emil Ludwig's biography was still available. In this memorandum I told Arthur that we should get a synopsis of this and outline our ideas to you. My memorandum stated that it could certainly be a big subject.

On May 21, 1956, James Mason wrote Kramer and me that he was still thinking about this for Magnani.

On February 21, 1957, Arthur Kramer wrote you and me a memorandum advising that we were in priority on the title and stating that the Rider Haggard novel would be a good springboard for the film. I asked Arthur to circulate this novel to all the producers, which he did on March 27, 1957.

The subject remained in abeyance until we had a creative staff meeting with you in July of 1958, following which we authorized our London office to buy the Rider Haggard novel for £1,000. This purchase took place on August 1, 1958.

As recently as September 2nd, 1958, I received the following cable from Darryl Zanuck:

"Many thanks for your suggestion of Cleopatra. Am very interested and have asked Dick [Zanuck] to bring script and all available material to me in New York Friday as possible DFZ Corporation project."

The script referred to was the scenario of our old picture.

In a memorandum to you of the same date I write as follows:

"I think Zanuck is the logical producer for this big subject. We have Brackett working on one costume spectacle and Engle on another. I can think of no one else on our list who can handle this type of subject. We have discussed and discarded Mervyn LeRoy as a prospect and I know Robson does not want to take on any historical pictures. At any rate, it looks as though you may have a customer for CLEOPATRA."

On October 16, 1958, you wrote Lew Schreiber as follows:

"Inasmuch as Wanger is going to start on Monday, October 20, I am officially assigning him as producer of CLEOPATRA and we will take over from him the deal that he made on the CLEOPATRA story with the English people."

In Schreiber's note to Ferguson dated October 20, 1958, the following appeared:

"In connection with the deal we made with Walter Wanger Pictures, Inc., Mr. Wanger brought to our attention that his company has an option on a project called THE LIFE AND TIMES OF CLEOPATRA, and he paid 4,000 pounds. We agreed that we would take over this project, which we intend incorporating into our own CLEOPATRA story, which will be produced by Walter Wanger Pictures, Inc."

There is no possible question in my mind that CLEOPATRA would have been made by this company without Mr. Wanger's interest. It was a very active project long before he came to this company and we were merely shopping for the right producer. When Wanger indicated that he had a CLEOPATRA book, inasmuch as he was just joining the company, we let him take over production of this subject. It was not his book – a research tome – that revived our interest. Far from it.

D. B.

1958: Sep 30

Wanger had option on [Cleopatra] book by Carlo Franzero. Wanger's first meeting with Skouras in New York.

1958: Oct 20

Wanger's first day at 20th Century-Fox studio.

1958: Oct 22

Wanger discusses <u>CLEOPATRA</u> project with Buddy Adler. Following actresses proposed: Joan Collins, Joanne Woodward, Suzy Parker.

1958: Nov

Skouras sees CAT ON A HOT TIN ROOF.

1958: Nov

Wanger claims he approached Elizabeth Taylor. Claims he called Martin Gang and Kurt Frings, Taylor's lawyer and agent.

1958: Dec

Ludi Claire assigned to assemble material and prepare rough script for CLEOPATRA.

1959: Feb

Wanger claims that following performers were considered by casting department for CLEOPATRA roles:

Cleopatra	Caesar	Antony
Joanne Woodward	Lawrence Olivier	Richard Burton
Joan Collins	Cary Grant	Burt Lancaster
Elizabeth Taylor	John Gielgud	Anthony Franciosa
Brigette Bardot	Yul Brynner	Kirk Douglas
Marilyn Monroe	Curt Jurgens	Marlon Brando
Jennifer Jones	Fredric March	Stephen Boyd
Kim Novak		Jason Robards Jr.
Audrey Hepburn		Richard Basehart
Sophia Loren		
Gina Lollobrigida		
Susan Hayward		
Dolores Michaels		
Millie Perkins		
Barbara Steele		
Suzy Parker		

1959: Mar 4

Nigel Balchin engaged to prepare screenplay from Ludi Claire's outline.

1959: May 27

[Wanger to Adler and Schreiber]

Wanger states his reservations re Mamoulian as director of Cleopatra; states that Mamoulian is slow in terms of technique and likely to create difficulties with desire of Skouras that film be shot as soon as possible; Wanger suggests that Henry Hathaway may be better choice as director.

1959: Jun 15

Skouras dines with Rouben Mamoulian and Gina Lollobrigida; discusses CLEOPATRA.

1959: Jun 19

Preliminary production cost estimate for CLEOPATRA based on Nigel Balchin's script: $2,955,700 (without cast or director).

1959: Jul 29

Nigel Balchin script submitted to Kurt Frings, as agent for Elizabeth Taylor and Audrey Hepburn.

1959: summer

[Adler to Skouras]

we want to start our picture in October and we have tried every possible means to obtain services of Hepburn or Taylor and have been unsuccessful.

1959: August

[Adler to Skouras]

Had another meeting with Paramount re [Audrey] Hepburn and absolutely no chance getting her. Tried again with Elizabeth Taylor; she would not talk to us unless we considered one million dollars against ten percent of gross. Tried making other offers to her but she refused. I emphatically turned her down and am proceeding to close with Lollobrigida.

1959: Aug 12

[Adler to Skouras]

Re Lollobrigida her agent advised that our proposal of $250,000 plus 5 percent of the gross after breakeven is unacceptable to her. As you know they asked us to stipulate that her 5 percent participation would commence after picture grossed six million and we have insisted that this 5 percent cannot commence until the picture break even and this is the stand I intend keeping.

We are still looking for an unknown for the role of Cleopatra. I honestly feel, Spyros, that if I continue to look and test we might come across the right Cleopatra and we then could make the picture for possibly a million dollars less than we could make it with Lollobrigida. I am becoming more and more convinced that "Cleopatra" the title is the star unless I had the biggest star in the business. This production might be just the one that would give us the opportunity to do what you mentioned previously, "to free ourselves from the bondage of the kind of deals the agents and actors are demanding." I will speak further on this situation when you arrive back in the country.

Most anxious to see you. My very best,

Buddy

1959: Aug 28

[Skouras to Adler]

Dear Buddy: Pursuant to our conversations regarding the telegram which you will send us for the sale meeting announcing the search for "Cleopatra," "Ruth," and "Theseus" in "The King Must Die," I had a meeting yesterday with the advertising and distribution departments in which we discussed this matter.

They were excited and highly enthusiastic over the idea which would not only give us several new talented personalities, but would give the pictures great celebrity and set them up as major productions because of the world-wide publicity linked to the talent hunt.

We think that the announcement of the talent search should be made as soon as possible and we would like to present the idea at our sales meeting, which starts Tuesday, as that we can inspire the men attending to participate in its operation fully.

Therefore, we would like to have a wire from you which we can present at the meeting describing the talent hunt and outlining the reasons for the search and the requirements for the roles. These, naturally, will be incorporated in the press announcement form you inaugurating the search.

Your press announcement should point out first that there is no one in Hollywood to qualify for the roles of "Cleopatra," the most alluring, provocative and desirable woman of history, or "Ruth," the noblest and most self-sacrificing heroine of all time. In Theseus we seek the epitome of manhood, someone almost God-like, since the story suggests that he was a descendant of the gods.

I am sure that your research department will be able to supply the physical requirements of the actresses and actors playing the roles, the coloring of eyes, hair, the fact that they must speak perfect English, their previous schooling, dramatic experience, etc. We ought to list the combination of talents and attributes which we are seeking to be embodied in our Cleopatra, our Ruth and our Theseus.

The announcement from you that Hollywood cannot supply the Cleopatra we want should make big news, and though we mention that we are looking for a Ruth and Theseus we should concentrate first on Cleopatra and the follow up with the other two.

If you agree with this, I think we should have the press break on Wednesday which will follow the presentation of your wire to the meeting on Tuesday. I think the talent search will do far more to give the pictures prestige than they would have with name stars in the lead.

It will also provide and excellent device for attracting new faces who can be important stars of tomorrow. Once we announce the search we can coordinate the operating of the casting department and the domestic and international publicity organization to give it a continuing buildup.

Kindest regards.

1959: Sep 1

Elizabeth Taylor in London making <u>SUDDENLY LAST SUMMER</u>; Wanger claims she told him by phone she would make <u>CLEOPATRA</u> for a million dollars.

1959: Sep 27

Meeting at Studio Sunday afternoon.

        Present: Spyros Skouras
                             Buddy Adler
                             Lew Schreiber
                             David Brown
                             Sid Rogell
                             Robert Goldstein

Discussed responsibility of Goldstein under new concept of British production; Goldstein responsible for production of <u>CLEOPATRA</u>; while Wanger may go abroad on the project, Goldstein responsible for all decisions, Adler to arbitrate any dispute.

Estimated cost of <u>CLEOPATRA</u>: between $4,500,000 and $5,000,000.

Rouben Mamoulian proposed as director.

1959: Oct 5

[Skouras to Adler]

Dear Buddy: Since our telephone conversation Saturday and Sunday regarding "Cleopatra" and the failure of the negotiations with Elizabeth Taylor and in accordance with our understanding to discuss the matter with you today, I had an extensive meeting this morning with all New York executives, including Murray Silverstone and Alex Harrison, and presented to them all details for their advice and recommendations.

Murray and Alex, as well as everyone of the executives, regret that the negotiations with Taylor collapsed but they strongly recommend – and this includes myself – that we should start production of Cleopatra as soon as it is physically possible with Susan Hayward, with the exception of Charlie Einfeld who would prefer an unknown. If you personally recommend an unknown it would be agreeable to us provided we don't lose any time.

Our telephone conversation this morning occurred while the meeting was in progress and everyone joins with me in urging no to delay the "Cleopatra" production.

In spite of this we recommend that if you can get Taylor to agree to three pictures at $2,100,000, or since you are sure that Columbia offered $2,500,000, we should meet that, provided that immediately after her MGM picture is completed "Cleopatra" be the first picture and a second picture, that we are to choose, to follow "Cleopatra." The third picture to be made after a reasonable time. In other words, the first two pictures back to back, or, if she objects to three pictures, then two pictures at one million and a half, provided they are produced back to back immediately after the MGM picture.

Or you can offer her one million dollars to star in "Salambo" immediately after she completes her MGM picture. Everyone feels that one million dollar investment for "Salambo" will be more justifiable than for "Cleopatra." As I told you before, practically everyone, with the exception of Charlie Einfeld, believes that Susan Hayward will gross in "Cleopatra," in the domestic and foreign markets, within practically the same amount as Elizabeth Taylor and the difference of the gross will be about what will be the increase in the cost of production, because of Taylor's salary and the necessity to produce the picture overseas and the double studio overhead, etc.

Dear Buddy, everyone here is cognizant of your exacting job and has full appreciation of all the difficulties and problems which are associated with the present terrible casting situation and our suggestions are only intended to be of service to you and to the studio and to inspire you in reaching the best conclusions for all of us.

Affectionate regards.

Spyros

1959: Oct 6

[Skouras to Adler]

Dear Buddy: As I promised you last night, in spite of the fact that you stated it was not necessary, I checked again with Alex Harrison and he told me that the difference of the grosses between Susan Hayward and Elizabeth Taylor in "Cleopatra" would be between $1,000,000 and $1,500,000, maximum.

Murray reiterated that the difference for the foreign market would be slight and in his opinion, it would not be over $500,000.

Regards.

Spyros

1959: Oct 7

[Adler to Skouras]

Re "Cleopatra" I note that Murray Silverstone and Alex Harrison state that Susan Hayward in "Cleopatra" would gross in the domestic and foreign markets practically the same amount as Elizabeth Taylor and the difference in the gross would be the increase in the cost of production because of Taylor's salary and overseas production. It would possibly mean that all we would do in the world would be $2,000,000 more with Elizabeth Taylor. I do not agree with Murray and Alex. It is my opinion that Elizabeth Taylor would gross a great deal more than Susan Hayward would, but I have great respect for Murray and Alex and in view of my respect for their judgment I go along wholeheartedly with their recommendation.

Regarding the Elizabeth Taylor situation and our most recent offer of two pictures, "Cleopatra" and "Requiem for a Nun," at $750,000 per picture against 7½ percent of the gross, we will not hear from her until around three o'clock today our time. It is my opinion that she will not accept the deal. Should she not I will so advise you but at the same time I will proceed with Susan Hayward as we cannot afford any further delay.

My very best,
Buddy

1959: Oct 8

Wanger claims Skouras wants to announce Susan Hayward for role of <u>CLEOPATRA</u>.

1959: Oct 10

Negotiations in progress between Kurt Frings and MGM re <u>Butterfield 8</u>.

1959: Oct 14

[Adler to Skouras]

Dear Spyros: We have concluded an arrangement with Elizabeth Taylor to do "Cleopatra" immediately following completion of the Metro Picture which is presently scheduled to start the first week in January. She agreed to accept $750,000 against 10 percent of the gross. Would appreciate your getting me Executive Committee approval as soon as possible.

For your information we got Walter Wanger to reduce his profit participation from 15 percent to 10 percent.

My very best,
Buddy

1959: Oct 14

[Skouras to Adler]

Dear Buddy: The Executive Committee and everyone here in New York appreciative of your wonderful patience and perseverance in handling the difficult negotiations with Elizabeth Taylor, her agents and her court.

Everyone insisted upon the date and since our telephone conversation I told them that the date is on or about April 20th.

Again congratulations. We are all very happy with the results of these very trying days and I am confident that you will produce a great box office attraction.

Affectionate regards
Spyros

1959: Oct 21

Rouben Mamoulian engaged as director of <u>CLEO-PATRA</u>.

1959: Nov 25

Dale Wasserman hired as writer.

1959: Dec 2

Wanger and Mamoulian go to London to look over facilities at Pinewood.

Skouras and Adler arrive in London to inspect Pinewood facilities.

1959: Dec 7

Elizabeth Taylor in New York convalescing from double pneumonia.

1959: Dec 8

Skouras and Adler return to New York from Europe.

1959: Dec 30

[Adler to Skouras]

When we made the deal on Elizabeth Taylor we had been advised that she would start Metro picture first week in January and was to start Cleopatra no later than April twentieth and we so provided in the contract. We were advised by Metro today that they have been delayed in starting their picture with her and their present plan is to start shooting on February 15th. This means that we will not be able to start with her in Cleopatra until around May twenty-third but please bear in mind that we may be delayed a bit longer if Metro has any further delay in starting their picture. My very best

      Buddy

1960: Mar 7

Johnny Johnston and John De Cuir visit Turkey to explore with Turkish Government the shooting of exteriors in Turkey. Conclude that Turkey not feasible.

1960: Mar 8

Consideration given to making <u>CLEOPATRA</u> in Italy with Lionello Santi (Galatea Productions).

1960: Mar–Apr (6 weeks)

Mamoulian visits Italy to inspect facilities with Santi.

1960: Apr 11

Laurence Durrell engaged to prepare script.

1960: Apr 20

Decision not to make <u>CLEOPATRA</u> in Italy with Galatea Productions. Determined that film will be made at Pinewood Studios.

1960: May 3

Wanger arrives in London.

1960: May 6

Memo from Adler to Wanger states limit on <u>CLEO-PATRA</u> budget is $4,000,000.

1960: May 14

Mamoulian arrives in London.

1960: May 19

Starting date determined by Studio as August 15.

1960: May 19

[Fathy Ibrahim (Cairo) to Skouras]
reminds Skouras of "the desire of the High Official to lift the ban on Liz Taylor's pictures and take her name off the black list. This only as a personal favour to you when they understood that our company had assigned her to play the leading role in our production CLEO-PATRA," which "will automatically lead to similar steps in all other Arab countries"; repeats that "the desire still exists but will only be done for 'Mr. Skouras' and not for any other person or company."

1960: Jun 4

Budget estimated at $5,000,000.

1960: Jun 10

[Adler to Skouras]

Dear Spyros: I was quite shocked and amazed to hear that Miss Elizabeth Taylor called you personally to make certain demands upon us re the role of Caesar at the same time criticizing our choice of Stephen Boyd for Antony and insisting upon Rex Harrison for Caesar. The studio has been working on this project for over a year and our investment will be close to $5,000,000 and possibly more. Unless the studio can produce this picture without the interference of Miss Taylor or anyone else there is no assurance that we can deliver this production at a cost that will make it marketable.

You also advised me on the phone it is your opinion that if Miss Taylor wishes her release from this project we should give it to her because with her attitude we would find ourselves in a very disastrous financial position because of her unrealistic demands. If this is your decision I am in full accord with it. Please advise what action is being taken.

In view of the above and assuming that Miss Taylor withdraws I am now investigating what our investment in "Cleopatra" is to date. In my opinion, and this is only a guess, we have over a million dollars already invested. We must immediately find another Cleopatra as we must maintain the same schedule we had set up for Miss Taylor so as to protect our below the line investments. It is vital that you notify me immediately upon receiving a release from Miss Taylor so that we can pursue a replacement. My very best

Buddy

1960: Jun 13

Wanger claims Skouras telephoned from New York
and called him a saboteur.

1960: Jun 22

[Wanger and Mamoulian to Skouras]
Re enthusiasm over Cleopatra project; "we are going
full speed ahead"; states costumes and dialogue in process of completion of being revised for Todd-AO.

1960: Jun 24

[Skouras to Adler]
Dear Buddy: Was delighted talk with you last night and
happy to hear your voice sounded stronger, in fact it
was almost back to normal.

Strongly urge that when you leave hospital, you
should remain home sufficient time to enable you re-
gain your strength. You can arrange have some meetings, but do not overdue it, and you should not have
too many telephone conversations. Your health is most
important and should be considered above anything
else.

My meeting last night with Mr. and Mrs. Fisher,
at first, was very disagreeable because she insisted upon
discussing specific scenes pertaining to production.

I have been consistent in my discussions with
her and told her that when you requested that we engage her for "Cleopatra," you asked for a budget of
$4,000,000 and secured the approval of the board.
Then later, after your first visit to Europe, you requested that "Cleopatra" be made in Todd-AO, therefore
you wanted to increase the budget to $4,800,000 but

you assured us that it would not exceed $5,000,000, and your statement was so recorded in the minutes when this was presented to the board.

As I informed you previously, I told her that you are ill and in the hospital, and that you are the only one with whom she can discuss this matter. I repeated this again to her last night. After a great deal of unnecessary talk, she became rather agitated and critical of me, then I told her that after she speaks to you if she is not satisfied and would like to be relieved from this picture, she would not have any trouble with us in this respect.

She stated that she would like to read the script and if she does not like it, she would not make the picture. I then replied that I would not blame her because I would prefer that she stepped out of the picture now, if she is dissatisfied, because I would not want her to be in a picture in which she did not have her heart.

She did not like my attitude and stated "I don't need you," and I replied "neither do we need you."

In other words, I did not allow her to place me in a position of having made any promise to her, but gave her to understand that you are the only man who can do anything you desired concerning this production.

With regard to the locations, I told her what you told me that, if necessary, the first unit would go on location and that it would not have to be Italy, and she agreed. I told her that perhaps it would be in Egypt, or Syria or Arabia, or any other place and she appeared to be calm when I made this statement to her.

However, she does insist upon reading the script. Therefore, please be prepared to have one sent

to her as soon as possible. She plans to be there within
a week.

I am sending you this information, so that you
can be further informed.

With my warmest wishes and may God bless
you and keep you well. I sincerely hope you will follow
my advice and not go to the office soon.

Spyros

1960: Jun 25

Skouras arrives in London.

1960: Jun 27

Skouras holds press conference in London. Wanger
claims Skouras fell asleep three times.

1960: Jun 27

Matters for discussion with Mr. Adler on the telephone
this evening (June 27th)
CLEOPATRA.

On my arrival here I met with Bob, Walter
Wanger and Rouben Mamoulian and with Feldman
drove to the hotel and we spent until five o'clock in the
morning discussing this subject and everybody under-
stands each other now.

Walter was under the impression that it was a
whim of ours not to make the film in Italy. He did not
realise that it was necessity and a matter of cost and
that as an Italian picture we had to turn it over into the
hands of an Italian producer and he would be supreme.
Even Mr. Adler could not interfere with his decisions

even if he wanted to. However, he now knows the reason for taking the film out of Italy and building the sets of Alexandria and the Forum in Rome in England.

Everybody is now in accord with the procedure and production is going ahead. In Todd-AO at a budget of five million dollars.

Durrell finished writing the script last Saturday and it is now being put into shape by Mamoulian and Wanger and will go into mimeograph in the next couple of days. You should have three or four copies in Hollywood by the end of next week.

No Caesar has been selected. Mamoulian and Wanger will meet with Sir Ralph Richardson to discuss the story with him and see if he will agree to play the part. Richardson has just finished "Exodus" and is now in Nice and they will fly down for a day to talk to him and get a decision. No other actor of importance and stature is available at the present time to play the part of Caesar. Production of the picture is still scheduled to start on August 15th.

1960: Jun 28

"CLEOPATRA"
MEETING
held at 31 Soho Square, London, W. 1.
4:30 P.M., June 28th, 1960

Present: MR. SPYROS P. SKOURAS
                  MR. ROBERT GOLDSTEIN
                  MR. ROUBEN MAMOULIAN
                  MR. WALTER WANGER

1. IT WAS AGREED that the Budget and all financial matters, as well as contact with New York and Los Angeles, should be channeled through Mr. Goldstein to Mr. Buddy Adler, who is the final authority, creatively and as to budget.
2. IT WAS AGREED that every effort must be made to produce the picture for not more than a Budget of Five Million Dollars.
3. IT WAS AGREED that in order to justify Todd-AO that in the event proper locations are not available for the desert sequences in England, proper locations will be found for the First Unit elsewhere.
4. With regard to the script, a cable has already been sent to Mr. Buddy Adler informing him that Lawrence Durrell has finished his writing of the script, which is now in the hands of Messrs. Wanger and Mamoulian, who are now cutting and bridging scenes eliminated and also numbering scenes, and the script should go to be mimeographed by the end of this week.

1960: Jul 13

Buddy Adler dies; Goldstein appointed head of the studio.

1960: Jul 15

Wanger writes lengthy letter to his lawyer, Gregson Bautzer, relating events, describing budget revisions, etc. States that they are "going around in circles, mostly due to the fact that Skouras and the Studio would refuse to read any reports, made not by Mamoulian and myself, but by the production staff hired by the Studio." Further states that Skouras "is still adamant in his insistences that exteriors of Rome and Alexandria will be shot in England." Further states he has "tried to discuss these matters with Skouras. He refuses to listen to them. As a matter of fact, he wouldn't even discuss these matters." Wanger further states that reasonable budget would be $6,000,000, rather than $4,000,000 or $5,000,000.

1960: Jul 16

Wanger appointed head of Fox European production, replacing Goldstein.

1960: Jul 18

[Wanger and Mamoulian to Skouras]
re proposal that Curt Juergens be cast in role of Antony; Wanger recommends that Juergens not be hired and suggests several alternatives.

1960: Jul 19

Skouras and Wanger meet in Athens, then go to Egypt.

1960: Jul 20

[Nita Arthur to Skouras, July 14]
Skouras visits Egypt accompanied by Walter Wanger and his daughter, and second unit director Andre Marton; Minister of Education and National Guidance Dr. Okasha gives dinner in his honor and orders that "all facilities and help be extended regarding shooting *Cleopatra* local location sequences also arranged with Army

officials making available as many soldiers and cavalry
as possible when filming."

1960: Jul 27

[Wanger to Mamoulian]
Wanger gives extensive criticism of the Durrell script,
stating that the historical impact has been lost in a "bu-
colic, domestic, provincial picture of the nature of 'Our
Town.'" Wanger suggests revisions in script to accord
with various dramatic ideas which he presents in memorandum.

1960: Jul 28

Wanger in New York re Elizabeth Taylor's contract.

1960: Jul 29

[Goldstein to Lew Schreiber]
Dear Lew:
          Received the following cable from Ernie Hold-
ing:
          "Am extremely concerned about position Cleo-
patra. Budget on new script excluding any desert locations with limited allowance for action sequence and
trick work still comes to approximately five million dollars. Sets will be ready for shooting August 15th but to
date no casting concluded, consequently costumes not
manufactured. Everything now held up whilst reconnaissance party comprising Mr. and Mrs. Mamoulian,
Miss Wanger, DeCuir, Hilyard and Joseph exploring
possibility of major first unit location Egypt and Athens. Understand Wanger proceeding New York today

to finalize position with Elizabeth Taylor. It is now obvious that main shooting cannot commence August 15th and that budget will exceed five million dollars. Would stress fact that any delay starting beyond August 15th entirely due to indecision regarding artists etc. as all problems construction draughtsmen, etc. in London now overcome."

Am at a loss to understand Walter. It appears clearly to me daily that Walter is deliberately trying to complicate matters so that the picture will definitely not start shooting on August 15th. Holding's cable clearly states that there are no problems now securing laborers, plasteres, etc.

Also, have talked to Holding on the phone today and am appalled that no casting has been done on this picture because long before I left London I had been after both Wanger and Mamoulian to cast the picture, see people, interview them and set them for an August 15th starting date.

Wanger and Mamoulian both looked at Scofield film while I was in London and I have been after them constantly to make a test of him regardless of the film which they had seen and they both promised that they would do this but have vacillated and surreptitiously avoided instructions to make this test. As a result we now find that starting time is now closing in on us, as you and I understand, and Holding states, we cannot delay the starting of this picture. Unless by rearranging cross-plot so that Wanger and Mamoulian can find work to do with Taylor and other members of the cast without Finch before September 15th, thereby avoiding any unnecessary additional expense, we cannot afford to wait for Finch. But, in any event, this picture must start on August 15th.

Have just received script from Mamoulian. This picture has had nothing but one delay after another and we are now getting to the point where it must start and August 15th is the date Mamoulian must start shooting. In talking to London today am advised that reconnaissance tour mentioned in Holding's cable has now been postponed because of them not being able to obtain visas and they are trying to leave next week. Please instruct Wanger that this reconnaissance trip will further delay the picture and as he has been to Egypt he can convey to them the information needed. In my opinion there is no need for them to make this trip but to instead concentrate on getting picture started in London on August 15th.

Understand that Mamoulian wants to rent a house requesting us to pay for it, claiming that the allowance agreed upon is in addition to the cost of the house. Told Copley that the allowance of seven hundred dollars weekly covers everything, but the most frightening thing to me is wanting to rent the house for a period of ten months. If Mamoulian is thinking of the length of lease in terms of how long it's going to take to complete this picture, and if Wanger has a similar kind of thinking, I think something must be done immediately about straightening them out.

I am frightened as to what this picture will ultimately cost at the rate Wanger and Mamoulian are procrastinating. So you must impress upon Wanger the importance of this picture starting shooting August 15th.

1960: Jul 28[?]

New starting date determined as Sept. 25.

1960: Aug 8

[Wanger to Skouras]
encloses information from Reader's Digest and
UNESCO re proposed filming in Egypt; Wanger emphasizes importance of this data and advantages of
filming the picture in Egypt.

1960: Aug 11

Elizabeth Taylor signs contract.
> Terms: $125,000 salary for 16 weeks.
>> $50,000 per week after 16 weeks.
>> 10% of the gross.
>> $3,000 per week living expenses.

1960: Aug 13–24

[Fathy Ibrahim (Cairo) to Skouras, August 18]
Wanger, Mamoulian and their team visit Egypt; Dr.
Okasha expresses delight with Skouras' decision to include "Nubian monuments in Cleopatra and making
special trailer for theatres also about Akhnation Nefer-
titi ... He immediately gave his full support and his top
advisers to assist in guiding and organizing everything
to insure practical success to our location problems and
enthusiastically offered ships and transportation whenever needed particularly Luxor, Asswan and all facilities
under his control which included making props and anything else he had in his organization."

London production (1960–61)

1960: Aug 31

Elizabeth Taylor arrives in London.

1960: Sep 6

Wanger relieved as head of Fox European production.

1960: Sep 7

[Rogell to Skouras]
reports start date December 12 for the Egypt shoot; expresses concerns with the first unit's increase shooting period in Egypt to six and a half weeks (with Taylor working one week less) which was excessive compared to the original plan of four weeks and her ten day schedule for shooting the same scenes in Italy. "I realize we have to take full advantage of the magnificent scenery, but I thought they had scheduled too generously and the cost would be exorbitant." Wanger and Ruben "were amenable, and we reduced the Egyptian location approximately to one month for the first unit, with Liz to be there about two and a half weeks." Rogell also announces the elimination of a $200,000 shooting at Abu Simbel, whose gigantic Statues would be submerged upon the completion of the Asswan dam.

1960: Sep 13

[Skouras to Wanger and Mamoulian]

Skouras states he is "downhearted" on reading Cleopatra scripts; asserts the importance of intimate love
scenes; real entertainment value in dialogue between
Cleopatra, Caesar and Antony; states he is anxious to
read new script.

1960: Sep 16

[Mamoulian to Skouras]
Mamoulian states that Skouras' cable expresses his
conception of Cleopatra; states he is constantly working on improving script; states he has many ideas re action and visual values outside the field of writing.

1960: Sep 14–26

Dec 27 1960
The following is a letter as if written to Mr. Koegel by
Mr. Lea of Joynson Hicks. The same has been seen by
and meets the entire approval of Mr. Walter Crocker.
"Dear Mr. Koegel
                         CLEOPATRA
        Together with Mr. Walter Crocker I saw Doc-
tor Vernon last night. The following are my notes of
the interview:
        Wednesday, September 14th. Doctor Vernon
summoned by telephone from the Dorchester Hotel
between 2 and 2:30 A.M. Arrived about 15 minutes later. Patient [Taylor] sitting up in bed short of breath.
Complained of palpitations of the heart and discomfort
in the chest. Said she had had similar attacks before.
Had been feeling quite normal on retiring to bed but
about three-quarters of an hour before, the palpitations
had started. Pulse about 180. Doctor Vernon explained

that at such a high pulse rate an accurate pulse count is difficult. Patient said "None of the usual tricks" worked in her case, such as pressing on the carotoid artery or pressure on the eye balls, but sedation had been given by her American doctor. Doctor Vernon spoke to patient's American doctor, Dr. Rexford Kinnemar, over the telephone. He believes but does not exactly recall that this call had been put through before he arrived. Dr. Kinnemar recommended sedation and in agreement with him Dr. Vernon gave patient an injection of ¼ grain morphine. He would not himself have used morphine if Dr. Kinnemar had not recommended it. After about 20 or 30 minutes no improvement in condition. Gave further injection of 3 grains of sodium gardinal. Pulse then gradually fell to 140. Patient said she was feeling sedated and thought she would be able to sleep. Dr. Vernon does not definitely recall whether the expression paroxysma tachycardia was used in the patient's presence but his impression is that the patient herself used the phrase without him first mentioning it.

Wednesday, September 14th. 11:00 AM. Dr. Vernon called on patient. Patient had slept for about three to four hours. Pulse reduced to between 130 and 140. Patient said she was feeling better.

Wednesday, September 21st. Dr. Vernon summoned by telephone. Attack much more severe. Pulse 190–210, patient insisted need for prolonged sleep. Injection of 2cc Peraldehyde.

Wednesday, September 21st. 11:30 A.M. Dr. Vernon called on patient. Pulse down to between 100 and 110. Patient feeling much better.

Wednesday, September 21st. 9:30 P.M. Dr. Vernon called again. Patient said she was feeling very tired. Injection given to make her sleep.

Thursday, September 22nd. Dr. Vernon summoned at midday. Patient complained of irritation on the lower and inner quadrant of the buttock. She thought it might be a bite. Dr. Vernon found a local inflammation which he considered might be the beginning of a boil. Prescribed an anti-inflammatory cream.

Thursday, September 22nd. 9:30 P.M. Dr. Vernon called again. Now clear that this was a localized infection and probably a boil, Kaolin poultices 4 to 6 times a day. Patient said she felt she was going to have a further attack of paroxysm tachycardia. Injection of sodium gardinol given. Patient tired and slightly hysterical. After consultation on the telephone with Dr. Kinnemar it was agreed that a course of pronestyl hydrochloride should be begun.

Friday, September 23rd. 12:30 A.M. Dr. Vernon summoned by telephone because of fresh attack of tachycardia. Patient or Mr. Fisher had already spoken to American doctor who had suggested two sedatives, one being tab. Attarax and the other phenergen. Dr. Vernon went straight to John Bell and Croydon in Wigmore Street and got these drugs on the way to the Dorchester Hotel. Patient very alarmed, tearful and inclined to hysteria. Pulse 180–190. Sedatives prescribed by Dr. Kinnemar. Administered by injection. Hysteria abated but tachycardia continued. Dr. Vernon states attack was less severe than previous attack and might be mainly an emotional upset.

Saturday, September 23rd. Afternoon. Dr. Vernon called again. Pulse rate normal. 72. Boil very sore but not yet fluctuant. Mr. Fisher without informing patient asked Dr. Vernon to call in the evening as he was worried at patient's drowsiness and unsteadiness in the evenings and thought that this might be the effect of the pronestyl.

Saturday, September 23rd. 10:00 P.M. Dr. Vernon called. Patient at first very angry at his arrival. Dr. Vernon had cancelled somewhat unwillingly a social engagement at Gatwick in order to do so. Was annoyed at patient's attitude and told her there were plenty of other doctors willing to attend her if she was dissatisfied with him. Patient mollified when Mr. Fisher assumed responsibility for calling Dr. Vernon and said she was quite satisfied with Dr. Vernon's treatment. Patient's pulse normal. Boil still very tender but not fluctuant. Prescribed Vitamin B and gave antibiotic injection of evromicene.

Monday, September 26th. Dr. Vernon saw patient at 1:00 PM. Boil more concentrated but still not fluctuant enough for opening. Temperature 97. No case of hysteria. Dr. Vernon advised an electro cardiogram to check that there was no injury to the heart and the making of a blood picture to check that pronestyl was not having side effects.

Dr. Vernon not surprised that when examined by Dr. Wilkinson on afternoon of September 14th patient was found to be fit. This quite normal in cases of tachycardia.

Dr. Vernon very unwilling to be drawn into matters of opinion but fully communicative and apparently frank of matters of fact. Dr. Vernon did not consider, however, that after an attack of tachycardia during the night, patient would have been really fit to answer an early call.

Patient on September 14th mentioned she had a medical examination for insurance in the afternoon. Dr. Vernon advised her to postpone it if possible.

Dr. Vernon not seen by Toplis and Harding but by Dr. Wilkinson and another doctor. Gave no written report or statement to them but gave them similar information to ourselves.

To sum the matter up, Miss Taylor had three separate attacks diagnosed as paroxysma tachycardia, the first being on Wednesday, September 14th, the second on Wednesday, September 21st and the third on Friday, September 23rd. There is a previous history of this complaint and it is vitally important that we should have the fullest information as to this. We require a full report from Dr. Rexford Kinnemar which should deal with the following points:

1. Does Dr. Kinnemar confirm the two telephone consultations with Dr. Vernon

2. Does he confirm the diagnosis of paroxysma tachycardia

3. Full details of his knowledge of the patient's previous history as to tachycardia with dates of every attack known to him.

We need from Miss Taylor a full statement also dealing in detail with the previous history as regards tachycardia and any comments on Dr. Vernon's version of the matter. Did any previous attack of tachycardia result in any interruption however short of her work on a film?

Both Mr. Crocker and I formed a much better impression of Dr. Vernon than we expected. Provided Dr. Kinnemar confirms the two telephone consultations we do not see much prospect of shaking him in cross examination. He does not exhibit any apparent animosity against Miss Taylor because he was discarded in favour of another doctor.

As a result of this interview I take a graver view of the situation than I previously did, but no final view can be formed without statements from Dr. Kinnemar and Miss Taylor.

The matter turns primarily on Miss Taylor's answers to Question 6A, 10A and 11A of the insurance declaration. See below as to question 6A. We must argue that paroxysma tachycardia is not a heart disease but is a condition not amounting to a disease. The answer to question 10A is crucial whether this was a defect to which she was subject and "Likely either temporarily or permanently to cause indisposition." I consider that "indisposition" must mean indisposition likely to interfere with the artist's work.

Mr. Crocker has seen this letter and suggests that I add, and I agree, that attacks after 14th September are not directly material unless Twentieth Century knew of them.

Yours faithfully"

P.S. Relevant questions on Hanover Insurance Company artistes declaration and medical report

6A   Have you ever suffered from a fit of any kind, diphtheria, meningitis, cerebral abscess, cerebral tumour, empyema, paralysis, gout, pneumonia, pleurisy, asthma, bronchitis, blood spitting or any chest disease, varicose veins, hernia rupture, rheumatism, tuberculosis, heart disease, diabetes, erysipelas, carbuncle or appendicitis, or from any nervous disease.

10A   Are you aware of any ailment or defect to which you are subject which is in any way likely either temporarily or permanently to cause indisposition or to affect your voice

11A   Are you perfectly well and in sound health.

Finis Metcalfe

1960: Sep 22

[Wanger to Skouras]

Lengthy telegram re many factors in Cleopatra shooting schedule; Wanger says he does not understand Skouras' surprise regarding rising costs; "if you will recall meeting with you and you staff in May all agreed that due to weather, labor shortages and inexperience in this type of production, costs would be greater in England and work would be slower than anticipated; notwithstanding all of this information, completely decided that large exterior sets be built at Pinewood and all interiors be shot here as well"; proceeds to discuss various items in budget: (1) delays in labor operation and labor shortages, exterior sets not yet completed; (2) casting Finch caused delay; (3) props, costumes and wigs were not ready; (4) set dressing problems and art costs up due to many items not properly executed; (5) weather delayed completion of exterior sets which could be shot now if they were finished; (6) miscellaneous account increase over unrealistic preliminary estimates; (7) script changes trying to meet budget requirements; (8) special photo effect; (9) cost of cast increased; (10) method of operation where production staff of Skouras' choosing operates without producer and director approving cost; reference to Taylor's schedule and 2nd unit's shooting schedule in Egypt; reference to time required for costume fittings and necessity to rearrange shooting schedule so as not to have shooting delayed by costume fittings."

Wanger … says all working full speed to start following Monday (Sept. 26) with Peter Finch in Caesar sequence so as not to be delayed by Taylor's fittings.

1960: Sep 28

Shooting begins on <u>CLEOPATRA</u> at Pinewood Studios.

1960: Sep 28

[Skouras to Wanger]
Skouras congratulates Wanger on Cleopatra starting shooting; includes Mankiewicz and latter's stop in London on way to Moscow; states that "regardless of whom you handle, Elizabeth Taylor or any great artists, they all need guidance and determined leadership."

1960: Oct 1

[Wanger to Skouras]
states that first two days rushes are excellent respecting various productions which Fox has in progress, with press releases annexed thereto.

1960: Oct 1–29

Elizabeth Taylor ill; does not appear on set.

1960: Oct 4

[Skouras to Wanger]
Skouras denies Wanger's statement that he "Skouras" made violent attacks against Wanger to Elizabeth; that

it is ridiculous; points out that Wanger was conscious of problems apparent in Italy and financial undertaking that would be involved there; living expenses; description of Italian producer; Skouras states that despite all these problems, Wanger insisted picture be made at least partially in Italy and this was the extent of Skouras' "attack" against Wanger in speaking to Elizabeth; Skouras states "let's avoid friction, have proven my confidence in you; now you must prove your regard for me; now give me the same consideration I am giving you."

1960: Oct 5

[Skouras to Wanger]
Skouras states he is airmailing comments re Cleopatra script which disturbs him greatly; encloses comments of his friend (unnamed in the letter [Mankiewicz?]) whose opinion is important because he has no axe to grind; annexed thereto is 3-page memorandum of comments on the script and suggestions as to revisions and development of principal characters; points out that he "Skouras" was insisting on intimate story with proper characterization rather than glamour; asked that part of script be sent to him; states that film can be shot as fast in England as anywhere else in the world.

1960: Oct 12

[Wanger and Mamoulian to Skouras]
alleged statement by Skouras that "he was thrilled about new scenes sent to him." Reference to Skouras comment on the script and his concern with it and hopes it will be improved.

1960: Oct 14

[Skouras to Wanger]
Skouras quotes wire from Lippert re film being made in Canada to demonstrate the excellent work that has been obtained from an English crew.

1960: Oct 18

[Skouras to Wanger]
Skouras' response to [October 12] letter. Skouras states he believes Wanger "misunderstood his remarks. He did not say he was thrilled with the new scenes but that it was an improvement over previous scenes; importance of making love scene more intimate and more human."

1960: Oct 18

[Wanger and Mamoulian to Skouras]
They have nothing left to shoot "because of Taylor's continued illness"; photographing exterior set despite weather; reference hairdressers strike and insurance problem.

1960: Oct 20

[Skouras]
Detailed description by Skouras as to his ideas. Skouras hopes for better picture through script as to the love aspect between Cleopatra, Caesar and Antony.

1960: Oct 29

[Wanger and Rogell to Skouras]

reference to rushes which were viewed; "Mamoulian said looked wonderful"; "trying to complete shooting but without jeopardizing quality."

1960: Oct 29–Nov 7

Elizabeth Taylor in London Clinic.

1960: Nov

[Nunnally Johnson to Goldstein]
I can never understand Wanger … Whenever I talk to him about *Cleopatra* he talks as if it were somebody else's production. Once I said to him: "Is [Taylor] due to work yet?" He replied "I hear she's overdue." What the hell does that mean?[1] (385)

1960: Nov 18

Production shuts down because of Elizabeth Taylor's illness.

1960: Nov 21

Skouras arrives in London; tells the press that CLEO-PATRA will be completed when Elizabeth Taylor recovers; is ready to fly to Cairo and meet with Egyptian government.

---

[1] Matthew Bernstein, *Walter Wanger: Hollywood Independent* (Minneapolis: University of Minnesota Press, 2000), p. 385.

1960: Nov 29

[Skouras to Wanger and Mamoulian]
Skouras advises as to his views on scene re protecting
of sanctuary at assassination of Caesar; says in present
form too academic and does not portray Cleopatra as
woman desperately in love with Caesar. Memorandum
annexed to the foregoing.

1960: Dec 4

[Wanger to Skouras]
advises several items re proposed Egypt trip; thinks no
one but Rogell should be sent because reorganization
so important and proper organization essential; reference to talks with Balchin regarding script changes.

1960: Dec 7

[Wanger to Skouras]
giving cost of operations for week December 10, December 31, total $276,765.

[Skouras to Wanger, undated]
re inquiry on exact date on which Taylor reports to
London.

[Wanger to Skouras, undated]
"Hughesdon calling you as no insurance coverage at
present for continuance of picture."

1960: Dec 8

[Wanger to Skouras]
stating Taylor should return ready for work January 3,
1961.

1960: Dec 9

Nunnally Johnson engaged to work on script.

1960: Dec 12

[Skouras to Rogell, Wanger and Mamoulian]
refers to recent description of the picture; Skouras cites
importance of principals and express view that "one of
the greatest pictures of all times possible artistically and
box office can be produced; needs polish. I think that
insurance brokers and underwriters will be satisfied
with assurance that Elizabeth Taylor will be reinstated;
lengthy discussion by Skouras of various scenes in the
picture and development of scenes of Cleopatra and
Antony.

1960: Dec 14

Joseph L. Mankiewicz sends his comments to Skouras
on the "Cleopatra" script. He estimates "a first cut of
well over three hours"; finds the script "shockingly bar-
ren of either scope or magnitude ... an opera without
music"; complains that it lacks the spectacular external
scenes of "Spartacus" and "Ben Hur"; and calls Cleopatra's characterization "as written ... a strange frus-
trating mixture of an American soap-opera virgin and
an hysterical Slavic vamp of the type Nazimova used to
play." However, he finds the combination of the three

characters "a brilliant idea, provided that a <u>new approach</u> is found for the telling," and offers a plot outline.

1960: Dec 19

[Wanger to Skouras]
re arrival of Taylor in London by December 17; states that if she arrived and tested, all testing would be out of the way before starting major production before January 3, 1961.

1960: Dec 28

Elizabeth Taylor returns to work at Studio.

1961: Jan 9

Skouras commissions Jack Brodsky to write an article for the *Arab Review* announcing agreement between the United Arab Republic and Twentieth Century-Fox to "perpetuate in a multi-million dollar film production program those moments of ancient Egyptian glory which the rising waters of Aswan Dam are not threatening with extinction ... Part of the arrangement with President Nasser calls for other film projects to be formulated there ... To make things complete ... President Nasser and the Government of the United Arab Republic have given Twentieth Century-Fox encouragement and cooperation which will not only mean a great deal to these pictures, but are certain to have a desirable effect on international understanding and friendship, and provide an inspiring example of the

most ancient art of our civilization being perpetuated
by the most modern of our time."

1961: Jan 14

[Rogell and Wanger to Skouras]
"Proposed plan for you close down here immediately;
start shooting with principals in Egypt about February
20; not maintain balance sets at studio while making
changes; 1st unit returns Hollywood and 2nd unit continues to Egypt." Further statement on commitment by
Taylor and her agreement to give Fox preference on future pictures, and Taylor's consent to "make personal
appearances all over the world with premieres of picture."

1961: Jan 15

[Skouras to Rogell and Wanger]
"Since arrival in studio have carefully analyzed studio
commitments which makes it impossible house production here. Therefore will do everything possible to
try start production [in London] as soon as possible."

1961: Jan 16

Meeting between Rogell, Wanger and Mamoulian in
which Rogell blamed Mamoulian for delays in resuming
shooting.

1961: Jan 18

Mamoulian resigns.

1961: Jan 18

[Skouras to Rogell]

Skouras approves sending $100,000 to *Cleopatra* unit in Egypt; also instructs to assign someone "in charge [of] expenditures and future money requests."

1961: Jan 22

[Wanger to Skouras]

describes in detail Wanger's grievance with Mamoulian; refers to script written by Lawrence Durrell under Mamoulian direction. Wanger states he could not get script from Mamoulian for a full week and then was disappointed when he read it and went with Mamoulian to meet with Durrell in Paris after Durrell was finished. Wanger states his fondness for Mamoulian but all efforts with Mamoulian were to no avail because of Mamoulian's demeanor. His demeanor is not that of a modern director ... the facts are that he was not ready to go ahead and shoot the very scenes he had complained of."

1961: Jan 23

Skouras asks for a detailed "Cleopatra budget for Egypt and purposes for which money will be spent"; Rogell estimates he needs $100,000 for the production in Egypt.

1961: Jan 25

[Mamoulian to Skouras]

Dear Spyros. Sorry must cancel today's flight. Azadia not sufficiently well for me to leave. Regrets and love from us to Saroula and yourself.

Rouben

1961: Jan 24

[Skouras to Mamoulian]

Dear Rouben. In keeping with our telephone conversation in order to relieve your mind from any anxieties concerning Cleopatra production your services will not be needed any further and are terminated as of this week.

Sorry hear Azeda still ill. Saroula myself wish her speedy recover.

Wish you best of luck for future. Kindest regards.

Spyros

Rome production (1961–62)

1961: Jan 25

Joseph L. Mankiewicz engaged as writer-director.

1961: Jan 26

[Skouras to Zanuck]
just signed with Joe Mankiewicz. he direct Cleopatra.
wanted you be among first know.

1961: Jan 27

[Zanuck to Skouras]
No matter how you look at it, this is an enormous improvement and if Joe is genuinely sincere he is capable
of doing a great job. I trust that he will collaborate with
Sidney Buchman on the script.

1961: Feb 1

Mankiewicz arrives in London.

1961: Feb 5

Sidney Buchman and Laurence Durrell begin working
on script.

1961: Feb 8

[Skouras to Goldstein]

Dear Bob: Regarding Johnny Johnston, it was not at my instructions that he be transferred to "Cleopatra" production, but when we were negotiating Mankiewicz's contract, he asked for Johnston and we agreed without knowing at the time that Johnston had been assigned to "Tender is the Night."

Although I know this may pose some difficulties for you, in view of our many problems with "Cleopatra" production, would appreciate your complying with Mankiewicz's request and making these arrangements, since he feels that Johnston is indispensable.

Please explain the situation to Henry King. Regards.

Spyros.

1961: Feb 9

Rogell submits budget report. Total cost to date: $4,998,000. Estimated further cost to complete picture: $4,866,000.

1961: Feb 17

[Skouras to Eddie Fisher]
Dear Eddie: Just learned about your operation; sincerely hope you are feeling much better and that your recuperation will be very speedy. Saroula joins me in extending heartiest good wishes.

1961: Feb 21

[Skouras to Ibrahim (Cairo)]

plans to visit Egypt on March 5, 1961 accompanied by
Mankiewicz, Taylor and her husband, and "probably
Wanger or Rogell."

1961: Feb 24

[Rogell to Skouras]
script progressing very well and I'm most enthusiastic
about what I have read.

1961: Mar 1

New starting date: April 4 at Pinewood.

1961: Mar 3–9

Elizabeth Taylor becomes seriously ill; taken to hospital; undergoes tracheotomy.

1961: Mar 14

[Eddie Fisher to Skouras]
Dear Spyros: Elizabeth and I just heard that you were
not feeling well and unable to come to London. Hope
you will be feeling better very soon. Warmest regards.
From Mark Anthony and me too.

1961: Mar 14

Decision made to suspend production in London and
start picture in Italy in September.

1961: Mar 15

[Goldstein to Skouras]

Dear Spyros:

Regarding "Cleopatra" personnel, it seems obvious that the only indispensable man from now until the time preproduction activities are resumed would be Joe Mankiewicz.

Regards

Bob Goldstein

1961: Mar 16

[Skouras to Eddie Fisher]

Dear Eddie: Throughout my lifetime have received numerous wires on various occasions inquiring about my welfare but none was more welcomed than one just received from Cleopatra Elizabeth and Mark Anthony my good friend Eddie.

Am feeling much better and love you both dearly.

Mrs. Skouras had many groups pray for Elizabeth and we are rejoicing at her recovery because she has so much to offer to world.

Our warmest wishes to you both.

1961: Mar 16

[Goldstein to Skouras]

Dear Spyros:

Kurt Frings came to see me and stated that the minute Elizabeth Taylor is physically capable of travelling she is returning to California and definitely will not return to Europe to work.

Feel you should have this information, because you will probably want to talk to Taylor or Eddie Fisher before tying up space for "Cleopatra" in Rome.

Regards

Bob Goldstein

1961: Mar 16

[Goldstein to Skouras]

Dear Spyros:

In view of the teletype I sent you today regarding Elizabeth Taylor, have gone over very carefully with Doc Merman and the production department the filming of "Cleopatra" here at the studio. We see no reason why, if everyone cooperates, this cannot be accomplished.

However, we must take into consideration that there is always the possibility that we will be losing the backlot, and we must also consider George Stevens' starting date, which, at the moment, is August. We do not know his requirements at this time but do know they will be on a big scale. Additionally, we do not know the status of the television production for the future. Also, as you know, we have an extensive schedule of our own shows.

However, if you feel that "Cleopatra" should preempt all other shows we will manage somehow to work out the schedule.

Would you please analyze the above situation, as I am sure you realize we are most anxious to cooperate.

Regards

Bob Goldstein

1961: Mar 28

[Goldstein to Skouras]

Dear Spyros:

Received following cable from Sid Rogell:

"All here still hoping make Cleopatra in Italy. Doctor Kennamer will advise within week or so if Taylor can work in Europe late Summer. Johnston Decuir with Wanger Mankiewicz exploring Italian locations this week following which Wanger returns London others check Egyptian locations for week or longer. Then all return Hollywood immediately via London unless decision made to produce Cleopatra Italy. Meanwhile everything possible being done reduce costs storing and packing for shipment designs sketches units costumes props wigs etc."

Regards

Bob Goldstein

1961: Mar 29

Elizabeth Taylor released from hospital; returns to California.

1961: Apr 18

[Skouras to Mankiewicz]

Dear Joe:

In order to approach the production, we must consider it in three ways:

a) From the economic point of view.

b) From the creative and artistic point of view.

c) From the entertainment and box-office point of view.

I would like to put forth certain views I have in mind for the purpose of impressing a greater impact on the public – beyond anything that has been done to date in any motion picture project, regardless of its size.

First, I would like you to supply me with some authentic footage – as it will appear in the picture – say about 1250 feet. My plan is to have demonstrations in 175 cities throughout the world – similar to the CinemaScope demonstrations. Invitations to these screenings would be extended to exhibitors, historians, clergymen, critics and newsmen, of course, in fact people in practically all walks of life. We will set up two or three of these demonstrations in every city, based upon the response to our invitations. I assure you that if this can be done, even the presently indicated phenomenal audience penetration will be augmented to greater heights than ever before achieved for any medium in the history of the entertainment world.

The plan is to hold simultaneous gala openings in 175 cities throughout the world. The sale of tickets will start six months in advance, on a reserved seat basis. I estimate the money we will receive from this sale of tickets will be .... (I don't dare to put it on record).

Therefore, with this plan you must approach this project courageously, completely disregarding the past; for any talk of past mistakes in the history of this picture is purely detrimental to the future reputation of this production.

As soon as you come to Los Angeles, I propose to start a campaign based upon Joseph L. Mankiewicz's name that will give new spirit to the production, and will convert defeat into victory.

This is the approach. But the plan I have regarding the simultaneous gala openings must be kept confidential until you, together with the cast and the executives of the Company, make the announcement about this great event in the motion picture world.

Therefore, we must take every precaution to see that the star's health is assured, and this I know is beyond anybody's power; but what I am trying to say is that we must take every precaution to produce the picture where Taylor will not be subjected to changes of climate and exposure to cold; and where her way of life is well regimented so that her health can be safeguarded.

At the same time, I must advise you that in this production the world will be looking for something unusual and out of the ordinary, because we will build up you and your name with such momentum that the audience will expect an extraordinary picture. Now this is the most dangerous part of the whole project – will you be able to give such a picture to the world … a picture that will fully reach the expectations of the people? If we achieve this, I can assure you that in the history of the motion picture to date no picture will ever be shown such attention.

I am giving you my thoughts on this in order for you to give me your reply. Naturally, your plans will be subject to Dr. Kennemar's advice; but if you set your plans, you will be followed by everyone and fully supported by me as well as by my associates. [draft of April 8: but in my experience, whether they are lawyers or doctors or board directors or motion picture directors, if you are the leader you will be supported. Don't expect anybody to tell you what to do, but you are going to tell them what is to be done after careful analytical approach to the project based upon the experienced assistance of the people of 20th Century Fox. We will meet and study your plans and I assure you they will be followed.]

Again, I would like to call to your attention that this is a dream I always had. I wanted first to put it into "THE GREATEST STORY EVER TOLD" (which I will do anyway), but I want to start this with "CLEO-PATRA," because of the great confidence and respect I have in your showmanship ability and your integrity as an artist dedicated to the greatest medium of entertainment in the world.

With kindest regards,

Sincerely,

1961: Apr 24

Wanger leaves London for California.

1961: Apr 29

Randall MacDougall engaged to work on script from Mankiewicz's outline.

1961: May 5

Wanger and Mankiewicz write lengthy letter to Skouras setting forth reasons why CLEOPATRA cannot be started until September, 1961.

1961: May 9–10

[Goldstein to Skouras]

Dear Spyros:

Regarding our commitment to Nunnally John-
son on "Cleopatra," I refer to your teletype of May 4th
reading:

"Dear Bob: You have not teletyped me concerning Nunnally Johnson and the work he is to do on
"Cleopatra."

Please clarify. Johnson was taken off "Cleopatra" in January and has no further work to do on that
production. Morris office here advises Lastfogel and
you agreed last week that our commitment to pay
Johnson $150,000 was to be settled by paying him
$50,000 now and $50,000 January 15, 1962, also
$50,000 now for his option to purchase "Twist of
Sand" for which he had paid 1,500 English Pounds.

Would appreciate instructions to pay Johnson
on foregoing basis.

Regards
Bob Goldstein

1961: May 12

[Mankiewicz to Skouras]

Dear Spyros:

I am quite frankly deeply disturbed and disheartened by
your refusal to approve Richard Burton as Mark Antony despite my most fervent urging. Certainly you must
agree probably the only problem we do not, repeat not,
have to face in the great task that lies ahead is that of
box office attraction in terms of cast name. There is
unanimous agreement, including yours often stated,
that Elizabeth Taylor in Cleopatra has become perhaps
the greatest pre-sold billing in the history of entertainment. To say that this could be damaged or even

dimmed by the presence of another name of possibly questionable box office draw simply cannot be argued.

Spyros, I have taken the most gigantic, the most difficult, and in many ways the most frightening undertaking of my career. I am only too well aware that it involves not only the creation of a great film but also the very existence of a great studio. I was aware of it when I accepted the responsibility in response to your urgings and to your often reiterated trust and confidence in my creative judgment as well as your often reiterated assurance of your full support in that judgment. Laurence Olivier and Richard Burton are my two carefully considered choices for Julius Caesar and Mark Antony. They are in my opinion the two greatest actors of this particular type in the world, and I believe further that the very announcement of their having been chosen will evoke an important reaction of delighted expectation from a world audience already almost too impatiently awaiting our film. If Olivier plays Caesar, then after his love story with Cleopatra comes to an end I cannot take the risk of loading upon the shoulders of an actor with less stature than his the responsibility for sustaining the entire second half of our gigantic film. Of the two great love stories we tell, that of Cleopatra and Antony is the one which scales the top-most dramatic and emotional heights. Of the two male roles Antony is by far the most demanding and difficult to play. Apart from his physical attractiveness and impressive personality, Richard Burton is a magnificent and experienced actor with the technical resources and dramatic power I can draw upon not only to sustain but to realize completely that all-important second half.

I know how many problems beset you at the moment and I, myself, begrudge the time taken from my literally day and night work schedule to compose this lengthy wire. My constant and keen awareness of your confidence in me has been a most important factor in the relentlessness with which I have been driving myself to accomplish this enormous obligation. You know that I am not given to frivolous requests. The production staff and your studio administration are in complete agreement with me that Richard Burton should play Mark Antony. There is a very good chance we will lose him unless we act quickly. I do hope you will withdraw your objection. Best regards.

       Joe Mankiewicz

1961: May 15

[Goldstein to Skouras]

Dear [Spyros]:

       Have just had a meeting with Joe Mankiewicz and his entire unit and find it is impossible at this time to give you even an estimated budget on the cost of "Cleopatra." To try to do a budget on the outline would only further delay the production of the picture as the entire production department would have to stop whatever they are doing in the way of preparation in order to concentrate on an estimated budget, which will be worthless.

       The script is now being written and many elements that are not in the outline will be incorporated in the script.

       Also, Mankiewicz, Johnny Johnston, John de Cuir and cameraman Bill Mellor are leaving on a reconnaissance trip to Rome and Cairo this Friday. Upon their return we can then get a more realistic estimated budget on this project.

Kindest Regards
Bob Goldstein

1961: May 15

<u>Press Release</u>
<u>(Peter G. Levathes)</u>

In a re-alignment of Twentieth Century-Fox studio operations, Spyros P. Skouras today announced the appointment of vice president Peter G. Levathes to supervise the operation of the company's studio facilities in Los Angeles.

Robert Goldstein, executive head of production, continues to be in charge of creative activities on the company's feature productions.

Levathes, who is also president of Twentieth Century-Fox Television, will continue to serve in that capacity in addition to his new duties, with headquarters at the studio.

1961: May 16

[Skouras to Goldstein (Las Vegas)]
Dear Bob: Please give the following wire to your friend Eddie tonight:

"Dear Eddie: All my heartfelt good wishes to you on your opening tonight. Wish we could be with you and Liz. Please give her all my love. Don't forget now I expect you to sing "Never on Sunday" like a good Greek patrioti. Remember: "Ap' to parathiro mou stelno ena kai thio kai tria kai tessera filia, pou phtanoun sto limani ena kai thio kai tria kai tessera poulia. Pos ithela na eho ena kai thio kai tria kai tessera pethia, pou san tha megalosoun olla na ginoun leventes yia hari

to Pirea. (Chorus) Oso ki'an psakso then vrisko allou
limani trello na mehi kani oso ton Pirea. Ki'otan vrathi-
azi louloudia m'arathiazi kai tis penies tou allazi gemizi
apo pethia." Yiasou Patrioti.

1961: May 17

[Mankiewicz to Skouras]

Dear Spyros: first of all my heartiest congratulations on
the well earned expression of confidence extended to
you [by the stockholders] yesterday. We are all highly
gratified and fervently hopeful that your time and ener-
gies can now be applied more fully where they are most
necessary.

Second, about Cleopatra. For almost a week
now, Spyros, our production planning has been sorely
impeded by the various departments struggling to come
up with a budget which could only be so premature as
to be totally worthless. How can a production be budg-
eted or even roughly estimated for which there is only a
general story line and no script whatsoever yet? Please
postpone your request for a budget at least until I have
returned from picking locations and have had a chance
to discuss the various departmental needs more fully
with the department heads concerned. I am very fearful
that to further distract the production staff from the
essential work they are now doing might result in delay-
ing our start.

Third, about Burton. Quite understandable you
could not let me know on Monday as you teletyped you
would. But time does grow short, Burton is in demand,
and we may lose him. Olivier is not available to us for
Caesar. I feel this makes it even more essential that we
have Burton as Mark Antony. I have been able to think

of no actor better qualified for the role in every way and more capable of providing the performance I will demand in the role as I conceived it. Best regards.

Joe Mankiewicz

1961: May 18

[Skouras to Mankiewicz]

Dear Joe: My Heartfelt thanks for your congratulations and good wishes on stockholders' meeting.

However, I am in need of your support, and of the support of many like you, to overcome my problems, which you know are plentiful, and "Cleopatra" is one of the many.

Am teletyping Bob the reply to your teletype in line with organizational procedure.

Regards.

Spyros

1961: May 18

[Wanger to Skouras]

Wanger states "how gratified everybody is" with results of stockholders meeting. "I am sure you are conscious of the unified ranks behind you that want to help make the future great for Fox and yourself"; refers to plans going forward re Cleopatra; states really first-class group of people are being gathered; reference to seeing Elizabeth and Eddie Fisher in Las Vegas.

1961: May 18

[Goldstein to Skouras]

Dear Spyros: Randall Mac Dougall completed two weeks services on script of "Cleopatra" for Wanger Productions on May 12.

We have until tomorrow, the 19th, to exercise our option for screenplay with compensation of $72,500 for 16 weeks of services.

We desire exercise option immediately. Please teletype executive approval today pending executive committee approval.

Regards
Bob Goldstein

1961: May 18

[Skouras to Mankiewicz]

This is the result of a most serious soul-searching deliberation on Richard Burton.

I called a meeting of our executives here in the advertising department and the sales cabinet of both the domestic and foreign, representing every part of the world, and everyone prefers Stephen Boyd; they strongly oppose Richard Burton.

From the arguments and philosophy expressed by these experienced men in the field, it is clear that they know Burton will give an accomplished, artistic performance but he lacks mass appeal, whereas Boyd will make a far greater popular emotional appeal compared to Burton's intellectual appeal, and the intellectuals are a very small percentage of the motion picture audience.

Up to this day, with the exception of "The Robe," Burton has never scored with a motion picture audience, whereas Boyd has won high acceptability and even so if he had not starred in "Ben Hur" and won tremendous critical approval, we would not be arguing for him.

We agreed with Joe on Laurence Olivier for Caesar and it is unfortunate that he is not available. But, in this instance, from the box-office point of view as well as the financial angle, it will be to the interest of the "Cleopatra" production, as well as to the studio, to propose Boyd. Since he is under contract to us and has such a great value, we would be under the most severe criticism and accusations if we went outside to take an inferior box-office value like Burton, and besides this will cost us three times the money.

In our own studio we have such a fine, appealing personality who, through his performance as Mark Antony, under the aegis of the capable direction of Joe Mankiewicz, can rise to the heights of stardom, based upon the inspiration and gifted handling that Joe will give Boyd.

I will wager both you and Joe that if Stephen Boyd was under contract to another company, we would pay a fortune to get him, just like Metro did everything possible to get him for "Ben Hur."

Therefore, I must say to you and Joe that I cannot, in good judgment, go against the opinion of everyone of my associates who with me will accept the responsibility for the "Cleopatra" project and who will give their faithful support to Joe Mankiewicz for this production.

Since I am morally committed to Joe, I would like him to consider this matter carefully. If Boyd did not score such great success in "Ben Hur" and as it is the most outstanding attraction in the history of the motion picture industry, then we would be justified in ruling him out. After thoroughly measuring the values between Burton and Boyd, I am confident that he will come to the conclusion that Boyd will excel from every viewpoint and will be of great benefit to the picture.

I regret that in spite of my announced statements that I would support Joe in all of his requests, which I intend to do if he insists, in this instance I want him to fully understand my position as president of this company and that the odds are so overwhelmingly in favor of our personality, Stephen Boyd, and that it would serve immeasurably to the success of "Cleopatra" and to the studio to cast him for the role of Mark Antony.

1961: May 19

[Skouras to Mankiewicz]

Dear Joe: Many thanks for your wire. I fully appreciate the position you have taken concerning Richard Burton and want you to know that we will abide by your judgment.

I want to do everything possible to help you in making the kind of a production that all of us anticipate and will give you my wholehearted support and cooperation.

Please try to make the right deal in securing Burton.

My heartiest good wishes for every success in this great undertaking.

Regards.

Spyros

1961: May 19

[Skouras to Goldstein]

... I hope that you will do everything possible to make the right deal in securing Burton for Mark Antony.

1961: May 20

Mankiewicz goes to Italy and Egypt to scout locations.

[Wanger to Skouras, undated]
stated Wanger has just read first act of Mankiewicz treatment which is "sensational, entertaining and exciting. I am sure we will get a picture that will gross $4,000,000."

1961: May 23

[Skouras to Wanger]
answering previous letter "I was very happy to read your appraisal of Cleopatra and about the plans now in progress. I fervently hope that everything will go forwards from now on and that a masterpiece will emerge from all the setbacks."

1961: May 25

[Levathes to Skouras]
... The only meeting [Goldstein] has called me in since I have been out here is at a meeting with Joe Mankiewicz when he insisted on a budget for "CLEOPATRA" and I went into Mankiewicz's office when he, Joe and Wanger were saying: "Spyros is crazy, how can we give a budget. What do you think?" I said, "I don't care how, but we must give New York a budget because the Board of Directors is asking how much is this picture

going to cost. This is a carte blanche – you cannot leave
New York without a budget." Joe is going to wire back
and say "I cannot." But I told them the more you say
you cannot, the more I think Spyros is right in insisting
upon it. You are in charge of the production – this is a
frightening thought. Are you going to spend
$15,000,000 – he said "no"; $1,000,000 "no"; well you
have a budget.

So, he called in Johnson and they turned it
over, and then he came up with $8,100,000 – but I had
to force him and he was fighting with Joe that New
York does not know what picture-making is and they
could not give a budget. It was good for them to get
some limitation on the budget.

1961: Jun 8

[Ibrahim to Skouras]
reports on Mankiewicz's visit to Egypt; "all facilities
have been extended to him and his party … a military
plane was put at his disposal with which he left for
Luxor and Asswan."

1961: Jun 12

Mankiewicz returns to California after scouting locations in Italy.

1961: Jun 26

[Wanger to Skouras]
reminding Skouras that he was to talk with Einfeld and
arrange for Ascelli to handle publicity for Cleopatra in
Italy.

1961: Jun 30

Decision to film ~~all~~ most of <u>CLEOPATRA</u> in Italy.

1961: Jul 26

[Mankiewicz to Skouras]

alarmed by rumors about Egypt's plans to nationalize industries, Mankiewicz urges the immediate reevaluation of "our entire Egyptian location ... if found necessary to abandon our projected work in Egypt an alternative must be created and put into work without the waste of an hour." Reports on his progress in Rome: "we are working here day and night trying to accomplish the impossible but even so have run into some unforeseeable delays such as uncovering of war shells bombs and mines and even the skeleton of a soldier while constructing Alexandria set. Thus we work not only with bulldozers but also with mine detectors. But each day brings us closer to realization of great film we all want and hope to live long enough to complete."

1961: Jul 27

Starting date for <u>CLEOPATRA</u> now September 18. Mankiewicz goes to Rome; Wanger remains in California for another month.

1961: Jul 28

[Goldstein to Skouras]

Dear Spyros

Will be with Mankiewicz in Rome Monday July thirty first Excelsior Hotel

Regards

Bob Goldstein

1961: Jul 28

[Skouras to Mankiewicz]

complains about the production's English accountant Sam Williams, whose "continuous doubtful operations ... also his regular fight and misbehavior with Egyptian crew [and] snobbish attitude towards Egyptians" caused the resignation of local production manager Gamal Madkour, "which will lead to uncooperative attitude with officials." Skouras recommends his removal.

1961: Aug 8

[Goldstein to Skouras]

Dear Spyros Have just returned from Rome everything production is progressing very well on Cleopatra. Mankiewicz due London Wednesday to finalise casting of all remaining parts. Strongly recommend that cast insurance be taken out on all important members of cast who are insurable and most important is insurance on Mankiewicz because in absence of a script and as entire production is in Mankiewicz's head it would be a disastrous loss if anything unforeseen should happen to him. Writing of script by Mankiewicz will be progressing throughout shooting period. Please advise regards. Bob Goldstein

1961: Aug 16

Executive Committee decision to postpone Greatest Story Ever Told.

1961: Aug 21

Peter Levathes cables Skouras: "have just received request for additional two hundred fifty thousand dollars from Rome for "Cleopatra," which makes total as of this date of almost one million dollars transferred with no shooting so far undertaken." Levathes urges Skouras to send a "top studio representative without delay to Rome [to] administer expenditure of funds."

1961: Aug 25

Wanger stops in New York en route to Rome; visits Skouras.

1961: Aug 27

Wanger arrives in Rome; crew of 100 technicians from Hollywood now in Rome.

1961: Sep 1

Elizabeth Taylor arrives in Rome.

1961: Sep 2

Skouras visits Rome; with Rogell.

1961: Sep 8

[Skouras to W. C. Michael, Executive Committee]
Dear Mike,

I have been here for a week, visiting the studio and having meetings every afternoon at 6:30 with Joe Mankiewicz, Walter Wanger, Sid Rogell, Johnny Johnston and others, and the main topic, of course, was CLEOPATRA: to have the script completed before they start production and, what is most important and necessary, to produce the picture at a reasonable budget.

Joe Mankiewicz has been religiously working every minute available on the script, although constantly interrupted by problems of casting, testing, production conferences and many other production activities.

After my strong statements regarding the budget, I repeated that without the finished script and final budget we cannot start production. Joe fully cooperated, by getting out the script to be studied by the departments which have to calculate the budget.

He delivered up to last night 212 pages and expects that the script, when completed, will be of about 275 pages. But if it was typed in the same way as the regular studio scripts, in my judgment, it would be of about 250 pages. He is to do additional writing for the dialogue.

I cabled you on my arrival here of my fears as to the production cost of CLEOPATRA.

As I described to you, the sets are breathtaking and overpowering and I have never seen their equal in my whole life. The entire preparation of the production is moving rapidly and I must confess that Joe has full realization of our problems, about the budget and also of Elizabeth Taylor being subject to sickness and, therefore, of the need to complete her part as soon as possible.

By doing this, however, while he will reduce the number of weeks she will work, he will prolong some of the other artists' shooting time.

I am glad I came here because I concentrated on Joe with all my strength and emphasized to him all our confidence on his having full realization and appreciation of all our problems.

His decision to send a second unit to Egypt and keep Elizabeth Taylor in one spot, so she will avoid the risks of traveling, is indicative of this full appreciation of his responsibility.

We have advised the boys to close all activities in Egypt until they are ready to start working there again with the second unit, which will be around January or February 1962.

Sid Rogell, since he arrived here, has acquainted himself with the production problems and can now start to be constructive. We had a meeting with Joe Mankiewicz, Walter Wanger, Sid Rogell and Johnny Johnston, and we agreed that Sid is to function through Johnston and not directly with the tradesmen because that might create confusion and demoralization.

Now that this has been established, I am sure that Sid Rogell is in a position to render precious services and help to speed the production.

I devoted all my time and, naturally, gave priority to the above subject. ...

I am looking to you to follow through in establishing the necessary economies in the organization that we discussed about. Also, I consider it advisable to establish that our people will travel by air, in the future, in economy or tourist class. If anyone should want to travel first class, he would have to pay the difference with his own funds. Furthermore, telephone calls should be reduced to the minimum. This is the first time I have been away more than a week from New York without making any telephone call.

1961: Sep 11

Rex Harrison engaged for role of Caesar.

1961: Sep 21

Skouras visits Rome; budget meetings with Wanger, Mankiewicz and department heads; budget $10 million.

1961: Sep 25

[Skouras to Wanger]
expresses "deep appreciation and thanks for courtesy extended during Skouras' visit in Rome." Skouras states he is "happy over the manner in which you approach the problems confronting the Cleopatra production in all that multitude and I would like to encourage you to bring about their solution."

1961: Sep 25

[Skouras to General El Sayed]
assures him "once again that our fervent hope is that CLEOPATRA will prove a great public relations medium for Egypt and will help acquaint the audiences of the world with the incomparable beauties of Egypt, her great antiquities and the magic of her climate."

1961: Sep 25

[Skouras to Wanger]
re cooperation offered by General El Sayed; points out it might save a great deal of money and increase importance of picture for it to be filmed in Egypt; requests Wanger's and Mankiewicz's reaction.

1961: Sep 25

Shooting begins on <u>CLEOPATRA</u> in Rome.

1961: Sep 26

[Skouras to Wanger]
Skouras extends "heartiest congratulations and appreciation" for Wanger's efforts in getting production under way: "Please convey to all members of the cast my fervent good wishes for a successful production."

1961: Sep 27

[Wanger (California) to Rogell (Rome)]
Listing 1st and 2nd unit crews sent to Europe on Ben Hur.

1961: Sep 28

[Wanger to Skouras]
thanks Skouras for very generous and thoughtful cable; refers to problems ahead with Elizabeth's help and states Bobby Lehman was impressed with this production; refers to enthusiasm of actors and anxiety to receive report from Levathes on first rushes.

1961: Sep 28

[Skouras to Wanger]
re proposed visit to Cleopatra set by Georgia Simmons.

1961: Oct 2

Rogell sends lengthy memo to Mankiewicz re various production problems and suggestions for cutting costs.

1961: Oct 2

[Wanger to Skouras]
re proposal for handling "Egyptian situation"; thanks Skouras for letter outlining cooperation offered by General El Sayed.

1961: Oct 4

[Wanger to Skouras]
re proposed visit of Georgia Simmons.

1961: Oct 6

[Skouras to Wanger]
Skouras stated he was "greatly impressed" by scenes witnessed; urges that every effort be made to reduce budget from $10,400,000 to $9,400,000; urges elimination of any scenes not absolutely necessary provided, of course, that such elimination of scenes does not imperil the quality and does not detract from the greatness of the picture … urges that every effort be made towards keeping the cost as low as possible.

1961: Oct 6

Skouras writes Mankiewicz commenting on portion of script sent him, suggesting revisions, etc.

1961: Oct 7–10

Peter Levathes visits Rome.

1961: Oct 18

[Wanger to Skouras]

refers to various production problems including weather but states "company is going to get tremendous attraction"; refers to shooting of precession scene; states "I think the entrance into Rome is going to be fantastic and one of the greatest things ever put on screen. Pete Levathes … has been of enormous help in coordinating some of our problems, and his counsel has been invaluable. I have great faith in his integrity, forthrightness and clear understanding of our problems and I am sure he'll reassure you as to the eventual success of the film."

1961: Oct 31

Skouras writes Mankiewicz commenting on further portion of script received.

1961: Nov 15

MATTERS FOR DISCUSSION WITH JOSEPH MANKIEWICZ

1) The company has extended itself in cooperating with you as to money and facilities – without any conditions – from the time that we entered into an agreement.

2) We have complied with your conditions, since entering into an agreement, and after the negotiations were concluded, you expressed your appreciation that you now

felt secure and were in the best frame of mind than ever before.

3) Ever since you moved to London, we complied with all the requests you made concerning the script, and engaged many writers. Naturally, we are rather bewildered that the script has not yet been completed, according to the statements made by you.

4) You insisted that the picture should be made away from Hollywood because the atmosphere and background of California were not conducive or in keeping with the scenic effects audiences would expect to see in "CLEOPATRA." If you will recall, at the time you stated that this move would help substantially to reduce the cost of the picture.

5) When you made the decision to move the locale of the production, you had full power. No one interfered with anything you did concerning all phases of this production. You were free in choosing your personnel, the sets, costumes, and even the cast.

6) We sent about 90 persons from the studio to Rome and took away the heads of each department at the studio in order that they may fully cooperate with you.

7) I am at a loss to understand what has happened with this production, because you agreed that we could start shooting September 18th. We therefore made an agreement with Elizabeth Taylor – in which you participated – for 8 weeks at a fixed salary, and for overruns, she would receive $50,000 per week. You stated that you would try to do everything possible to reduce the number of weeks for her services.

8) Up to this time, we have spent over $7,000,000 on the new CLEOPATRA version and based upon reports received from the studio, we do not have more than 15

minutes of film. This is a dangerous and critical situation, which must be corrected.

9) We must accelerate the production by putting at least two additional units, which I understand you are planning to do, and the picture should be completed by the end of January.

10) The length of the picture should not be more than three hours – or three and a quarter hours at the maximum.

11) Based upon the letter you sent me, dated December 14, 1960, you criticized the previous "CLEOPATRA" version of Walter Wanger and Rouben Mamoulian and stated that this was not the intimate story of Cleopatra and Caesar, and Cleopatra and Mark Antony. You stated that you believed the picture should be based on the intimate story and should not be a picture of big Italian mob scenes which practically every small picture made in Italy does have. Therefore, the new version should not have mob scenes. Yet, we have assembled the greatest number of people for scenes than any other picture ever made.

12) We should eliminate any questionable scenes, which you are taking for protective measures and which you feel are really not necessary. We should complete the [production] by the end of January; get through with Elizabeth Taylor as soon as possible because of the $50,000 per week and if necessary if there is anything missing, you can always shoot it later. By taking these steps we would be much better off than to continue with this production on the present scale.

1961: Nov 16

Skouras and Levathes visit Rome; budget conference; budget now $12,500,000.

1961: Nov 19

Budget meeting of all department heads at Skouras' suite at Grand Hotel; Wanger comments why all the hysteria.

1961: Nov 19

[Rogell to Skouras, November 22, 1963]
NOTES RE MEETING: SUNDAY, NOVEMBER 19, 1961
GRAND HOTEL – ROME
1:30 PM TO 8:30 PM

The following persons were present at the meeting:
S. P. Skouras
Peter Levathes
W. Wanger
L. L. Mankiewicz
Sid Rogell
Joe Di Muro – Attorney
Johnny Johnson – Unit Manager
Joe Popkin – Unit Manager, Second Unit
Rosemary Mathews – Production Secretary
Fred Simpson – First Assistant Director
Frank Maglia – Italian Unit Manager
Jack Smith – Head Art Director
John De Cuir – Art Director
Herman Blumenthal – Art Director
Paul Fox – Art Director

Leon Shamroy – Head Cameraman
Joe La Bella – Head Props
Ed Winigar – Head Wardrobe

Following a thorough discussion of costs, delays, etc., and future plans, Wanger made a remark to the effect that he saw no reason for anyone to get hysterical … whereupon Mr. Levathes became very angry and said it was time for someone to get hysterical, or at least show some real interest in the huge costs and many problems facing us. In other words, Levathes thought Wanger was entirely too complacent under the circumstances, and certainly didn't intend to apologize for being upset with conditions.

Popkin remembers distinctly that it was Levathes, not Skouras, who had the argument with Wanger.

Simpson attended the meeting but left early as he had the calls to make for the following day. Simpson remembers having heard of the argument the following day when someone told him about it on the set.

Leon Shamroy remembers the argument between Wanger and Peter Levathes which occurred at this meeting and is very clear upon the point that it was Levathes who was so upset and took Wanger to task when he mentioned "hysteria" or "hysterical attitudes."

Joe Di Muro remembers the meeting and the incident just as Shamroy does, i.e., that it was a heated discussion between Levathes and Wanger.

Leon Shamroy also says that he went to Walter Wanger, the producer, many times during the course of the picture regarding unnecessary sets which were being built, and that some sets were being built too large. He also did go to Mr. Wanger when parts of the script would come through and point out to him that certain

scenes were not necessary and should not be shot.
Shamroy says that nothing came of any of these suggestions and he can only assume that Wanger did nothing
about them.

1961: Nov 25

[Wanger to Skouras]
refers to complaint about unfavorable publicity; asserts
that publicity comes from Hollywood columnists that
"we financed to come over and really tell about the
film"; urges that "we cease spending money to get bad
publicity."

1961: Nov 30

[Skouras to Wanger]
Skouras points out that columnists when visiting set
cannot be sidetracked because favorable reports of the
columnists is very valuable.

1961: Dec 4

[Wanger to Skouras]
Wanger replies to Skouras letter of Nov. 30 re columnists; criticizes "catering to these scandal-mongers."
Wanger states that columnists are only interested in in-
creasing their own power by printing destructive items;
states that their subversive efforts undermining a great
industry; refers to persons who were successful without
catering to columnists; accuses Skouras of catering to
columnists; states each columnist causes great delay in
work; impairing efficient progress of the film; "there is

no way of treating them properly except ignoring them."

1961: Dec 5

After Sid Rogell's projected figures "shocked us all," Levathes decides to send Lawrence Rice to put expenditure under control.

1961: Dec 5

> [Levathes to Skouras]
> Dear Spyros: Re your exhibitor meeting, here are various items discussed with you on phone:
> [...]
> 4. Runaway production: we are opposed making pictures abroad except for artistic reasons.

1961: Dec 6

> [Skouras to Levathes]
> Dear Peter: many thanks for the suggestions for my speech. They are all constructive and valuable. I also like your telegram to Rogell, but I wish it were a little stronger. Do write him a letter and make it as strong as you can. Have you written to Joe Mankiewicz? Because you stated in your cable that you were writing.
> Kindest regards,
> Spyros

1961: Dec 13

> [Skouras to Wanger]

Skouras replies to Wanger's letter of Dec 4; emphasizes that when Hollywood columnists come to Rome regardless of how Wanger or Skouras feel about them they should be treated with the proper courtesy and not with hostility; Skouras points out that such columnists should be given attention regardless of who sends them and whether you or I like them and points out sums being spent to produce the class film we should bend efforts to create best publicity.

1961: Dec 14

[Eddie Fisher (Rome) to Skouras]
My Dear Spyros: Whatever happened to the Greek songs.

1961: Dec 15

[Skouras to Eddie Fisher]
Dear Eddie: Have not yet received songs. Will send them to you when available. My love to Elizabeth also to Cleopatra and Apollo.

1961: Dec 19

Larry Rice arrives in Rome to coordinate budget; estimates budget at $24 million.

1961: Dec 20

[Wanger to Skouras]
refers to Skouras letter dated December 13, 1961, and states that all visitors have been treated with courtesy and understanding; referenced to visit of Sheilah Gra-

ham states outstanding example of the "kind of person who should not be sent here." Wanger states the more of such people that can be kept away the better. When visitors arrive everything is done to placate them. Reference to Wanger's New York [Christmas] visit; states he saw three-quarters of an hour of film which is "absolutely out of this world. Joe has achieved a marvelous atmosphere and is creating a film of the intensity the like of which nobody has ever seen."

1961: Dec 26

Wanger in New York; attends meeting in Skouras' office. Present: Spyros Skouras, Walter Wanger, Joe Moskowitz, Otto Koegel, Peter Levathes, Don Henderson, J. Michaels.

Discussion of the $24 million budget figure given by Rice. Wanger claims the company executives tried to place the blame on Mankiewicz. (In fact it was Wanger who blamed Mankiewicz for exceeding budget.)

1961: Dec 28

Wanger returns to Rome.

1961: Dec 29

Skouras writes Mankiewicz commenting on portion of script for second half of CLEOPATRA received.

1961: Dec 29

[Skouras to Rogell]

Dear Sid:

I have received copies of your letters of December 11th and 13th, and am happy to hear that Larry Rice is now working diligently on the CLEOPATRA costs.

I am sorry that you are disheartened with the remarks in my letter of December 6th, particularly when I stated that you are there as an observer. But the second paragraph of your letter of November 30th to Peter implies that you had no responsibility for this production and blamed others for what happened, and I quote:

"The figures are shocking, but realistic, I believe. I don't know where the money had gone, but they have thrown away $5,000,000 ... sets too large and costly, everyone including actors here on salary and living allowances for weeks and months before they were needed. ...... the worst planning and management in the world ......"

Although I agree thoroughly with many of the remarks you make in your letter to me of December 12th, I want you to accept your share of responsibility and instead of criticizing and blaming anyone for what may have happened in the past, you should take immediate steps to correct any waste or mismanagement which is detrimental to the interest of the company.

Unfortunately, you were not connected with this production from the start, but you have been with it since the shooting began and have been with it now a long time. Therefore, steps should have been taken to remedy the situation.

When Walter met with us the other day, he said the "parent company in New York" was at fault and placed all the responsibility upon me. This is indicative of everyone's attitude that none of you are to blame. But, we have been supplying you with money, you have been spending it, we have acceded to all your demands for the personalities you have requested – yet none of you accept the responsibility for the mistakes that have been made, but try to put them on my shoulders. You feel self-satisfied and are absolved from any negligence or responsibility.

I know that you will tell me we gave Joe Mankiewicz full powers. It is true. But in my presence and in the presence of the heads of all the department, Joe stated that he did not want to take any responsibility concerning the production, but only for the direction, and that he wanted a man in charge of the various departments to be held responsible and to see that everything is ready when he starting shooting, so that he could shoot uninterruptedly.

It is not my intention to criticize you. But we are greatly concerned about the slow progress of this production, particularly since we have seen Joe's production "log," and I would like you to ask him for a copy of it. Joe complains that there is no one to help him, that the sets are not ready, the costumes delayed, etc. Therefore the shooting is progressing very slowly. He should be shooting at least 2½ to 3 pages daily and this should be your responsibility. I am sure that the sets are ready on time.

Joe is not a small-minded man. He is very understanding and conscientious about his responsibility. Although he is aware of the huge sums it is costing us daily, you should again bring this to his attention. Never before have we paid so much for any production.

With regard to the accusation you make that I gave instructions to Doc Merman to give Joe anything

he wants. Doc sent you a letter on December 19th clari-
fying this matter. I never told anyone that Joe had carte
blanche for this production or that he could proceed
without getting approval through proper channels. My
only intention at all times was to inspire him to do a
superb job.

I hope that meanwhile you are negotiating with
Mr. Deleani to see that we receive the best terms and
conditions for Cinecitta. Let me repeat that the statis-
tics show the cost for building in Italy is 36% to 40%
lower than it is in the United States, whereas our people made their estimate on the sets on the basis of 85%
of the U.S. cost. This figure is certainly out of proportion and you should negotiate the same terms the Italian producers receive. I know you can handle this very
capably and will succeed in getting the cost reduced
substantially.

Stop complaining and discontinue to blame
others. Correct the situation so that no one will blame
you. Don't only think of reducing the cost of transportation, but concentrate on ways and means to reduce
other expenses, particularly the shooting time. We must
shoot 2½ to 3 pages daily if we want to survive.

Peter is arriving there Wednesday morning. My
warmest wishes for a Happy and Successful New Year.

Sincerely,

Mr. Sidney Rogell

Excelsior Hotel,

Rome, Italy.

1961: Dec 29

Mankiewicz cables Skouras re criticism of his exceeding budget; offers his "complete understanding" if his replacement as director is under consideration.

1961: Dec 30

[Wanger to Skouras]

"Understand Einfeld in London; think it important for him come London and see assemblage of film to date."

1962: Jan 1

[Skouras to Mankiewicz]

Dear Joe. Mrs Skouras joins me in extending to you and your sons also your loved ones heartiest wishes for happy New Year. Confident Cleopatra will be world's greatest motion picture achievement.

Spyros

1962: Jan 2

[Skouras to Mankiewicz]

Dear Joe. Your cable December Twenty-ninth just received this morning.

Our purpose in phoning you was merely advise you of Peter's visit to Rome because of our anxiety increased by Walters report to us. As one associate to another tried explain to you my great concern prompted by prolonged shooting schedule.

There has never been any question in my mind regarding quality this picture but there must be some realistic relationship between quality and cost which I know you fully appreciate

Peter arriving Wednesday and will remain as long as necessary. Be helpful.

Happy New Year

Spyros

1962: Jan 26

Rumors re Taylor and Burton affair commence.

1962: Jan 30

[Levathes to Skouras]

Dear Spyros:

As of January 23rd we had 126 minutes of cut film on "Cleopatra." We continue to be of the opinion that this picture is meeting all our expectations. The performances of all artists are outstanding and Taylor, in particular, is giving a first-rate performance.

What continues to concern us, however, is Mr. Mankiewicz's refusal to cut down the script, for if we continue at this rate we will have a picture well over six hours to contend with when the time comes for final editing.

All efforts of mine, and now of Doc Merman's as well, have failed to persuade him to cut the script and reduce the running time. We shall continue our efforts with Joe and when he has finally completed the script, which should be within the next two weeks, we can then concentrate on cutting down the script and eliminating sequences which have not yet been shot.

Our best estimate for completion of photography in Italy is May 17th, assuming no interruption of the current schedule.

Regards.

1962: Feb 15

> Skouras writes Mankiewicz with comments on latest portion of script received.

1962: Mar 10

> Skouras and Otto Koegel arrive in Rome; episode of dinner with Simonetta.

1962: Mar 11

> Budget meetings in Rome.

1962: Mar 12

> Skouras, Otto Koegel and Wanger screen 2 hours 40 minutes of <u>Cleopatra</u>.

1962: Mar 21

> [Wanger to Skouras]
> Wanger reminds Skouras of several items discussed during Skouras' visit to Rome; (1) Film by Newsreel Department re enormous production problems facing current Fox productions with commentary by prominent exhibitor for use at shareholders meeting and to impress the trade; (2) that leading artists of every country be sought to do Cleopatra poster in important markets; (3) making of 35mm television film about the making of Cleopatra, with script by Randy MacDougall, who has worked for NBC; annexed to Wanger's letter is memorandum from MacDougall to Wanger, dated March 21, 1962, re making of television "spectacular" concerning the making of Cleopatra.

1962: Mar 22

Wanger claims that Skouras called him re sending letters to Taylor and Burton about their behavior; claims
he told Skouras not to do so and thus he "saved the
day."

1962: Apr 6

Skouras sends confidential letter to Mankiewicz re publicity over the Taylor-Burton affair; quotes press criticism; urges that Taylor's scenes be completed as soon
as possible.

1962: Apr 7

re departure of Jack Brodsky; tremendous amount of
publicity and need to affect foreign press; Wanger recommends that Brodsky be replaced by Nat Weiss.

1962: Apr 10

[Skouras to Wanger]
re award of "E" flag to Cleopatra; calls Wanger's attention to viciousness of Italian newspaper attacks and
states it is worse here "we must do everything possible
to bring about favorable publicity to overcome adverse
stories."

1962: Apr 12

[Skouras to Wanger]
annexing Wanger's letter of March 21, 1962, re television spectacular; Skouras states it would be mistake to
have such promotion scheme as not in keeping with

stature of the film; acceptance of such an offer would
jeopardize investment in Cleopatra; Skouras also states
that it would be a "mistake" for artists to do Cleopatra
posters as Wanger suggests; hopes that special reel can
be made for stockholders but stated nothing should
cause disruption of completion of film.

1962: Apr 13

[Skouras to Wanger]
Skouras states "It is most essential" that everything
possible be done to keep Elizabeth out of headlines in
view of publicity. Asked Wanger to impress upon Elizabeth importance of public appearance in Burton's
company. Desire to put a stop to abusive articles. Refers to Wanger's prior statements of his great affection
for Elizabeth and requests him to do everything in his
power to help her; suggests that Wanger should warn
and, if necessary, discipline Burton, impressing upon
him that he will succeed in destroying Elizabeth if he
persist in meeting her publicly ... Skouras includes a
number of quotations from articles in the press, all of
which are highly critical of Taylor and Burton ...
Skouras states that quotations reflect only a few of the
comments received and "we are quite disturbed by the
strong attacks against Elizabeth"; urges Wanger to ex-
ert every effort to avoid Taylor and Burton being seen
publicly: "She stands to lose a great deal if public opinion continues to stand against her."

1962: Apr 19–May 7

Elizabeth Taylor not working.

1962: Spring

<u>Wanger</u>: I talked with Joe and to Doc and as far as performance is concerned we have nothing against Burton. He showed up in good shape. You should talk to Kurt Frings regarding the girl.

I talked with Burton this afternoon and he is doing all he can to get the girl on the set.

I talked with Joe and he said I cabled Skouras that I will withdraw from the picture. Burton likes Joe very much. He thinks the world of him. I told him that Joe wants to quit and Burton was very upset and wanted to know whether there was anything he could do. He will see Joe this afternoon and will tell the girl.

<u>Skouras</u>: The studio will give a memo to Kurt Frings and I think we should also serve notice on Burton – to scare them.

<u>Wanger</u>: He was out only one day. I think we should not.

<u>Skouras</u>: We should discipline them.

<u>Wanger</u>: We have nothing against Burton.

<u>Skouras</u>: He has been drunk on the stage.

<u>Wanger</u>: There is no harm in disciplining him.

<u>Skouras</u>: We are mailing copies – the Studio is doing it.

<u>Merman</u>: While Walter was talking I remembered a man called Winston Churchill. During the war, when they were bombing England he said work, blood and tears. But in the end we will come out victorious. And I say to you Spyros, it will take a little longer but everything will come out alright.

<u>Skouras</u>: When I came there I came to encourage you.

<u>Merman</u>: You did a good job, Spyros. There are many complications.

I could write a book about Joe Mankiewicz, about everyone. But stop worrying. It will be alright at the end. You will be a great man.

1962: Apr 26

[Wanger to Skouras]

Wanger states "I feel as strongly as you do about the unfavorable publicity that Elizabeth has been receiving and have discussed the matter with her any number of times and also with Richard." States: "Nothing seems to stop Elizabeth at the moment. I am sure that the time is coming really soon when she listen to reason." States: "Situation more complicated than ever by arrival of Mrs. Burton." States: "We succeeded in giving out the story about her (Elizabeth's) nose which deflated for the moment the suicide story" ... reference to Richard Berlin's visit and proposed series on the picture, eliminating gossip and scandal ... Reference to viewing 3 hours and 45 minutes of first assemblage: "I must say it looks great and if can get the proper opening plus finishing Elizabeth I will feel much happier. However the impact of the picture is unbelievable." ... States that they are on the home stretch and hopes that by May 15, 1962, Elizabeth's key scenes will have been shot.

1962: Apr 26

[Wanger to Brand]

Wanger urges Brand to try and keep Sheilha Graham from coming to London because she will not be seen by principals which will naturally infuriate her and result in her printing all the gossip; states Graham's mate-

rial written on her last trip was unreliable and unfriendly "Skouras most anxious to send such gossip and personal stories in which Graham specializes"; states
"Have seen 4 hours assemblage of film which is magnificent and has tremendous audience appeal."

1962: Apr 27

[Wanger to Skouras]
re report on visit by Dick Berlin and his family enclosing letter by Berlin's daughter re desire to visit Cleopatra set.

1962: Apr 30

[Wanger to Skouras]
"unless you instruct otherwise will bar Sheilah Graham
from the studio as her stories have been so unreliable
and unfriendly to the corporation and our production
that I can only foresee further difficulties which your
recent letter stated you wished corrected."

1962: Apr 30

[Wanger to Skouras]
Wanger suggests that Screen Actors Guild write letter
to Taylor and Burton re their deportment, and that
SAG might be forced to take action. Says "I regret that
the Corporation did not, several months ago, send a
notification of this sort to Elizabeth and to Richard
when we advocated it after our first serious misadven-
ture with them." ... Description by Wanger of press
coverage and influx of screen and newspaper writers
from London, New York and Hollywood ... continues

discussion re future shooting plans and completion of
script ... Wanger states he ran 3 hours and 45 minutes
of film with Goldstein. "I cannot tell you how impressive this is even with this very long assemblage which is
not even a cut. The film is unique and must be compel-
ling and absolutely something the world has never seen
on stage and screen and with careful editing and with
the action scenes about to be put in, it should be an
overwhelming attraction for the next 40 years." ... continues description of forthcoming shooting of battle
scenes ... everybody including Joe has made a great
contribution ... Discussion re proposed deal with Sol
Hurok; continued statements as to how effective film
is; Wanger suggests Skouras come look at film before
stockholders meeting; states that even though no polishing, "but even in this state I find it has a tremendous
impact." ... "Sid Rogell, Doc Merman and Erickson
have done wonderful work since they've been here and
if we had had Rogell, Erickson and Merman from the
beginning we would not have had to endure what we
have suffered through" ... morale of company excellent considering what they have been going through."

1962: May 3

[Skouras to Wanger]
Skouras replies to Wanger's letter of April 30. Refers to
Wanger's statement that "they have violated and
breached their contract and that the costs to the Company have been enormous." Skouras states he is "glad
to know that you feel as strongly as I do about the unfavorable publicity that Elizabeth has been receiving,
and I am pleased that you discussed the matter with her
and Richard a number of times"; Skouras states he

wishes that Wanger and others with responsibility had taken as serious a view of Elizabeth's conduct as Skouras did when he first visited Rome and discussed it with Wanger. Skouras states he does not think we should stir up the Screen Actors Guild to make protestations; states that Wanger, the producer on the job, had "the primary responsibility of seeing that this picture proceeded according to schedule."

1962: May 4

[Skouras to Wanger]
re unfavorable newspaper publicity on Cleopatra; Skouras disturbed by Wanger cable re Sheilah Graham in which Wanger stated that Skouras was "most anxious to send such gossip and personal stories"; Skouras states never instrumental in asking any member of press to visit set; Graham started vicious column campaign when not treated cordially when she visited set; Skouras states he is not interested in inviting columnists on set.

1962: May 14

[Wanger to Skouras]
"Cleopatra truly unequaled in annals of show business ... public appeal surpassing anything put on screen ... Cleopatra has all ingredients demanded of biggest motion projects ... greater residual values right up to end of this century ... convey real assurance to shareholders. At last I can tell you that your convictions and supreme dedication to this production are finally on the home stretch. Warmest personal regards and thanks for your faith and support of Cleopatra."

1962: May 28

CLEOPATRA'S "death scene" filmed.

1962: May 30

[Wanger to Skouras]
re "E" flag.

1962: May 30

[Wanger to Skouras]
re completion of interior mausoleum and retake of film
ruined in transit.

1961: May 31

[Skouras to Mankiewicz]
Dear Joe:
On my visit to Rome with Mr. Koegel, I was told that
Miss Taylor's services would be completed in mid-May
and photography of "CLEOPATRA" completed at the
end of June. Upon my return to New York, Mr. Koegel
and I reported these facts to our Board of Directors.

Now we are informed there will be further serious delays and that Miss Taylor's services will be needed at least through July 4th. This is contrary to our
objective of trying to finish with Miss Taylor as fast as
possible.

These reports have been greatly disturbing to
me as they are at variance with what we understood
and what we reported to the Board of Directors.

As I told you at that time, we could not afford
any further delays because of the enormous financial
strain this puts on the organization, as the interest

charges alone amount to over $150,000 per month. And you were shocked by the enormity of the cost.

I am now in a hospital, on the road to recovery from an operation, and the news I have heard now of further delays, and the possibility that photography will continue well into August, have caused me the deepest concern.

After discussing this whole situation and our urgent financial requirements with all my associates, I find it necessary to direct that we terminate Miss Taylor's services not later than June 9th, 1962, and complete all photography on CLEOPATRA not later than June 30th, 1962.

There will be no monies available after those dates to pay for the services or expenses of Miss Taylor.

I am compelled to direct that payments to Mr. Wanger's company of compensation for services and expenses of Mr. Wanger terminate immediately.

I am asking our associates to deliver this letter to you, in the confident belief that you will be understanding and cooperative. If you could know how serious our situation is, I would not have the slightest doubt of your sympathetic and cooperative action. I am counting on you not to let me down at this vital moment.

With kindest regards.

Sincerely,

1962: Jun 1

Peter Levathes, Otto Koegel and Joe Moskowitz arrive in Rome; read to Wanger the Executive Committee order terminating Wanger's services.

1962: Jun 7

[C. Kurt Teutsch, Ph.D. to Skouras]

Dear Mr. Skouras:

Many thanks for your letter of March 30 in response to my telegraphic offer of assistance with Mr. and Mrs. Fisher. I appreciate and admire your explanation of your studio's position.

Thanks to my original and successful technique, which has enabled me to get quick results where other professionals using conventional methods had failed, I know I can be of value to you and your production staff in difficult personnel situations.

The delayed appearances and unauthorized absences of such stars as Miss Taylor and Miss Monroe have proved costly to your studio. For this reason you cannot afford to ignore my offer to be of service.

Why not let me prove what I can do for you? After only one session with me, I assure you, Miss Monroe will be ready and willing to return to the set on time.

I am ready to save you time, money, and trouble. Just give the word.

Cordially yours

1962: Jun 21

[Mankiewicz to Skouras]

Feel I must reiterate my considered professional judgment that executive committee's arbitrary decision to abandon final two days of essential silent shots of Taylor which link and support dramatic and emotional climax of entire film is decision of potentially inestimable damage to audience impact and understanding and therefore to success of film itself. Admittedly decision was reached without analysis by the committee of either film already shot or of script. As one intimately involved with both I urge reconsideration of decision to close her out this Saturday for sake of not only film but Fox itself which must secure greatest possible audience response and financial return for gigantic investment. For myself please be informed that under circumstances I must also reiterate that I cannot accept responsibility for proper editing or dramatic quality or even successful telling of completed story.

Contrary of whatever unqualified opinion you have received Cleopatra is not yet a finished film and abandoning it at the point of completion seems to me a most frivolous and destructive decision

Joseph L. Mankiewicz.

1962: Jun 23

[Merman to Skouras]

Dear Spyros I am sure that a great weight was lifted from your mind when you were told that the girl was officially finished. Believe me when I say that I too felt a great sense of relief.

ELIZABETH TAYLOR IN ITALY

Total Production days (No Sundays & Holidays)	226
Total Days no call	48
Total Days Worked	121½
Of total days worked Miss Taylor was late on 99 days (or a total of 53 hours)	
Total days she did not work	56½
Absent because of her fault:	34½
Illness	33½

Refused call		1
Cancelled because of	rain	3
	cold weather	1
	travel to Ischia	1
	Mankiewicz illness	2
days off per contract		3
Standby call – not used		2
Saturdays on 6 day week	10	22
		56½

1962: Jun 26

Skouras resigns as Fox president, to become effective Sept. 20, 1962.

1962: Jun 26

[Wanger to Skouras]

re 1st unit completed; Egyptian filming ahead of schedule; "confident film greatest box office motion picture."

1962: Jul 9

[Levathes to Skouras]

following blunders and problems with locals who "were trying to make a fast buck," it is decided that Fathy Ibrahim "will assume the entire responsibility of our operation in Alexandria prior to shooting during and after completion ... guaranteeing us no interferences from any sources whatsoever ... we do not use military personnel but civilian reserves." This includes "1508 Egyptian type men, 500 Roman type men 250 horses, 250 rider for 5,000 pounds per day" which includes everything except props and wardrobe, for four days. "Evidently our cancelling out of Egypt must have created a furor with certain higher ups as he has assured me that he will have no local government interference whatsoever ... the higher ups are most anxious to have us and will go all out in their cooperation assuring us there will be no custom delays, no red tape and that our operation will create no problems for us." Also announces the dispatch of equipment and the start of shooting within a week. "Aside from the publicity value this move to Alexandria at these prices is more economical than California."

1962: Jul 9

[Skouras to Ibrahim]
This important responsibility was assigned to you because of my faith in your ability and hope you will not fail me by having anything go wrong with production.

1962: Jul 12

[Skouras to Mankiewicz]
Dear Joe Appreciate your understanding financial responsibilities we facing your cooperative spirit and your efforts meet schedule. Peter advises rushes have been held at studio July third therefore strongly urge you return Hollywood immediately after Egypt. You realize our anxiety windup completely Cleopatra's overseas operation. Kindest regards
      Spyros

1962: Jul 15–26

Location shooting in Egypt.

1962: Jul 26

[Ibrahim to Skouras]

"Mankiewicz finishing first unit shooting today afternoon leaving with Wanger tomorrow for Rome." Second unit to finish shooting the weekend of the 29th. "Everything is very satisfactory and the appreciative cooperation of government helping making everybody pleased."

1962: Jul 26

[Skouras to Ibrahim]

my deep gratitude to government yourself for cooperation efforts towards satisfactory completion Cleopatra."

1962: Jul 26

Wanger sends cable to Skouras stating all photography is completed.

[Casting Budget]

	SALARY	LIVING EXPENSES
TAYLOR*	1,725,000	277,500
HARRISON	361,667	17,929
BURTON	479,667	28,514
McDOWELL	94,250	14,374
CRONYN	178,334	13,410
MANKIEWICZ	360,000	74,344
(VALUE (FIGARO) PURCHASE)	(347,282)	
	707,282	
WANGER (AUG 62 – JUN 62)	88,000	?
* EXTRAS PAID ALSO THRU HER CORPORATION MCL FILMS. S.A. ($140,000 plus $50,000 transaction)		
ESTIMATED DAILY COST IN ROME: $125,000 230 DAYS @ 125,000 = 28,750,000 in Italy (no Egypt or Spain)		

Postproduction (1962–63)

1962: Aug 9

[Levathes to Skouras]
Dear Spyros:

As of June 1961 the studio payroll consisted of 2154 people exclusive of the laboratory. Tender is the Night was the only picture on the studio stages at the time. Since June 1961 the following pictures were started: Comancheros, The Longest Day, State Fair, Cleopatra (latest version), Young Man, The Lion, Mr. Hobbs Takes Vacation, Nine Hours to Rama, Five Weeks In a Balloon, Something's Got to Give, Woman in July.

As of August 4, 1962 the studio staff had been reduced to 606 people exclusive of the laboratory, following termination of principal photography of Woman in July and return of the Cleopatra company from Rome.

The roster of producers on June 1961 which stood at twenty-nine including special commitments with Charles Feldman, Seven Arts, etc., has been reduced to fifteen.

The forty-one writers employed on thirty-one projects in June 1961 have been reduced to nine writers on nine projects.

In June 1961 the studio had fifty-five players on the weekly contract list at salaries totaling $26,995 per week. This contract list has been reduced in the interval to twelve people with salaries totaling $7,480.

Closing of the talent school in June 1961 also resulted in savings of $678 weekly.

As of July 1, 1961 the studio contractual commitments totaled $15,651,477. As of June 30, 1962 the-
se commitments have been reduced to $12,216,728, a
reduction of $3,434,749.

Estimated overhead for the year 1962 has been
recomputed since last April to reflect what the overhead would be for one year from July 1962, based on
production conditions as they exist now. The forecast
shows the overhead to be about $7,500,000 instead of
$9,500,000 for the year starting July 1962.

Regards
Peter

1962: Aug 31–Nov 7

[Zanuck to George Sidney, President, Directors Guild
of America, November 7, 1962]
Dear Mr. Sidney:

As a result of irresponsible statements that have
appeared in the press in connection with the alleged
"termination" of Mr. Joseph Mankiewicz's services as
the director of "CLEOPATRA," I feel compelled to
write to you as President of DGA in my capacity as
President of Twentieth Century-Fox Film Corporation.
Every statement that I make in this appraisal is factual
and can be documented.

First, I would like to advise you of the splendid
experience I had recently with another member of your
Guild. I refer to Mr. Mark Robson. Mr. Robson has
completed a magnificent film titled "NINE HOURS
TO RAMA" which he produced and also directed for
his own independent Red Lions Films Ltd. for Twentieth Century-Fox release. I would like to emphasize the
point that Mark was not only the producer and director

but he has an independent Corporation with a financing and distribution contract with Twentieth Century-Fox.

Mr. Robson came to New York to screen for me his film. I made certain editorial recommendations and suggestions. At first Mr. Robson did not agree with my views. Nevertheless, he followed my recommendations and made all of the changes that I had suggested. Once again, we worked on the film in London and Mr. Robson voluntarily adopted my reconstruction of the continuity and the eliminations I felt should be made. These eliminations amounted to a total of approximately twenty-four minutes. We worked harmoniously, and while at times we disagreed, we were both completely satisfied with the final results.

I hasten to add that I did not find it necessary to "save" "NINE HOURS TO RAMA." It would still have been a splendid film without any of my recommendations but I am certain Mr. Robson is grateful for whatever contributions I may have made. In any event he so expressed himself.

Our relationship was on the basis of mutual respect and it was never necessary to air any "grievances" in the press. Mr. Robson voluntarily terminated his services when the job was done.

This leads me into a quite different situation in connection with "CLEOPATRA" and to begin with I must state that Mr. Mankiewicz's services commenced January 31, 1961. His contract called for a 40 week guarantee which expired on November 6, 1961. His contract was terminated on the completion of his work in Paris which was approximately eleven months beyond his contract completion date.

Mr. Mankiewicz was engaged as the director of the film (and not the producer). He was also engaged to "supervise the re-writing of the scenario." He was at all times a paid employee of Twentieth Century-Fox.

His contract states as follows: ("We" refers to Twentieth Century-Fox and "Artist" refers to the director.)

"We agree to consult with the Artist, at reasonable times with respect to the creative elements (including major casting and editing) of the Picture, but if we do not mutually agree with respect thereto, it is understood that the decision of our then Executive Head of Production shall be final and conclusive; provided, however, that if our then Executive Head of Production is away from our studio for any reason, then he shall have the right to designate another at our studio to make the required decision with respect to the foregoing."

In addition to the above the contract also specified that the "Artist" shall have the right to make the first cut of the picture, subject however, to the following conditions:

"That neither Figaro, Incorporated (the Mankiewicz Corporation), nor the Artist, shall be entitled to any compensation for cutting services rendered by the Artist after the end of his guaranteed period of employment; and (ii) that the completion of the Picture shall not thereby be unduly delayed."

This is the legal aspect of the situation. Under the contract Mr. Mankiewicz's services could have been terminated eleven months ago. Irrespective of the fact that the contract clearly specifies that he shall not be entitled to "any compensation for cutting services," Mr.

Mankiewicz was carried on the payroll until October 27, 1962.

This brings me to the "moral" aspect of this highly publicized "controversy" in which I have been publicly accused of usurping the "unfinished" work of an "Artist." I refer you now to a letter I wrote to Mr. Mankiewicz on August 31, 1962.

"Dear Joe. This letter is dictated in Paris, but by the time you receive it I will already be back in New York at the home office.

At the last meeting of the Executive Committee of the Board of Directors, I was questioned in detail about the status of "CLEOPATRA." Since I was not familiar with the actual facts, I deferred replying to them but will of course make an official report at the next meeting.

I would like to see your completed "first cut" of "CLEOPATRA" no later than the first week in October. I assume that by that time you will have eliminated any obviously unnecessary footage (if such exists) and that in the meantime you will send me a progress report indicating the approximate "completion dates."

I am writing this letter to you but I have no objection to you showing it to Walter Wanger or to Stan Hough or to Bobby McClean.

I have no intention of jeopardizing the quality of what most certainly must be a great artistic and commercial achievement, but as President of this Corporation I cannot ignore the absolute necessity of completing the editing, special effects, music, dubbing and re-recording as soon as possible.

It is inconceivable that I shall desire to injure or depreciate the ultimate value of this film, but at the same time it has become a problem that I have inherited, and am now responsible for.

The Board of Directors have pointed out to me some very startling figures. Between now and the release date, Twentieth Century-Fox is paying interest on the money we borrowed from the banks to make and complete this film. The <u>interest</u> costs us $7,000 per <u>day</u>. This, of course, is added to the negative cost. In addition to the above, if the negative has not been cut, the prints made and the film sent out of California by the early part of 1963, we will have to pay a California State tax amounting to more than $700,000.

This all boils down to one fact – in addition to the 28 employees who are now on the completion of "CLEOPATRA," and in addition to your salary and their salaries, it costs us $7,000 per day to operate.

I am not at all worried about meeting the California tax date, as I am convinced that there is no logical reason why the film cannot be completed and the negative cut long before this date, but I am concerned about the matter of daily interest on the loan. This is cash that goes down the drain and adds nothing to the quality of the film itself.

I have been told that you have expressed the "fear" that I will take over the project and edit it myself. This will not occur as long as I am satisfied that proper progress is being made. If I am convinced that progress is not being made, then of course I have no alternative but to exercise the authority and responsibility given me by the Board of Directors.

From a personal standpoint, I am eager to see the film. All I have heard about it has been exceptionally good."

In reply, Mr. Mankiewicz expressed complete satisfaction and in his letter he included a mimeographed copy of the Completion Schedule which he had prepared with the production manager Doc Merman and the head of the editing staff, Barbara McClean. This report is as follows:

Finish Editing	October 15th
Dupe to Music	October 15th
Dub Dialogue	October 20th
Combine Dialogue & Effects	November 10th
Start to Re-record Final 6 Sound Track	December 11th
Start Cutting Negative	December 20th
Ship Negative to New York	February 29th

You must bear in mind that this report was sent to me by Mr. Mankiewicz. I call your attention to the first item titled "Finish Editing."

On September 12, 1962 I sent the following telegram to Mr. Mankiewicz:

"Many thanks for your letter of September fifth. I am studying the problem. Pending seeing the film I agree that overall length should not be in excess of four hours and apparently now it runs approximately five and one half hours. Will it be approximately four hours when I see the first cut early in October. It is obvious that nothing much can be done by the other departments including dubbing until we reach the four hour mark therefore our most vital problem is to complete the first cut so that the other departments can begin to function and so that we can prepare the dubbing schedule. The footage that you eliminate should be assembled by Dorothy Spencer so that I can review the eliminations after I have seen your completed first cut."

Mr. Mankiewicz completed his version of the film and arrangements were made to assemble the cast in Paris to dub various episodes. The dates for this work were prepared at the Hollywood Studio and approved by Mr. Mankiewicz. It was arranged that I would see the film in Paris prior to the commencing of the dubbing. The actors were assembled in Paris with fixed starting dates. Among others the cast included Elizabeth Taylor, Richard Burton, Hume Cronyn, Gregoire Aslan and a number of supporting players. Again I wish to emphasize that it is normal and common practice in this industry to avoid dubbing or obtaining "wild lines" until the editing of a film has been completed. Mr. Mankiewicz endorsed this basic principle in writing and this is why in spite of urgency I permitted his additional time to complete his cut of the film and although the contract did not call for it, I instructed that he be kept on payroll until the dubbing was completed.

Mr. Mankiewicz completed photographing the film in Rome on July 28, 1962. He reported to the Hollywood Studio on August 2, 1962. He spent a total of 5 or 6 weeks editing and completing his version of the film. He arrived in Paris on October 11, 1962. He screened the film for me in Paris on October 13, 1962.

The film ran, when I first saw it, four hours and thirty-six minutes. At my request the cutter, Dorothy Spencer, had brought to Paris approximately 40 minutes of scenes that Mr. Mankiewicz had eliminated, but I was surprised to learn that he had not brought the dubbing "loops" for these eliminated sequences. It is obvious that Mr. Mankiewicz considered his version of the edited film "completed" or he would have brought with him the "loops" for the eliminated sequences as they involved the same actors that were to be in the other sequences. On this point I refer you to a paragraph from a letter sent to me on September 5, 1962 by Mr. Mankiewicz from Hollywood covering this specific point.

"We have a rather large amount of 'dubbing' to do. Naturally, it would be foolhardy and expensive to undertake this until the film is at least roughly an approximation of its eventual length. Also, with very few exceptions, all of the actors needed are abroad. We think it would be most practical, therefore, to set up a concentrated 'dubbing' session in London on or about October 20th. This will necessitate locating the needed actors and having them in London on the specified date."

After seeing the film twice as well as the eliminated sequences, I wrote the following letter to Mr. Mankiewicz on October 20, 1962:

"Dear Joe. I have not been idle on CLEOPATRA. If I have been 'inaccessible' since I first screened the film it is because I have been devoting myself almost exclusively to a study and analyzation of the film. I should complete the preliminary stage of my 'Study' tonight or tomorrow morning.

I have taken the pains to not only study every line of dialogue from the screen, but also from the script, in an effort to evaluate what could or what should be done from the standpoint of editing, reconstruction and the possibility of extensive Second Unit operations, as well as the possibility of several important retakes.

The two previous letters that I sent you should indicate the extent of my concern of the physical aspects of the film. You do not quarrel with them.

You reference to am as 'the newly-elected President of a gigantic Corporation' etc. is accurate, but my approach to this gigantic problem has been the approach of a practical film producer who has inherited the most expensive and the most 'mis-produced' motion picture in film history. This probably sounds immodest, but had I been in on the project, as you say, 'from its inception,' we would not be facing the acute problems we face today. This, of course, to a degree, is 'second guessing,' but in this case the production errors were so obvious that you yourself, in your letter to me, indulge in it.

I consider it fortunate in one respect that I was not in on the project from its inception. I am not wed to anything except what I see on the screen. I am not interested in the past, on why 'such and such' was done or wasn't done. I am not even interested in who was or was not basically to blame.

In my opinion, we have all of the elements of an outstanding and great production that will, to a certain degree, have a chance of justifying its cost. Much is left to be done, not only from editing and reconstruction but in the reorganization of the undeveloped or only partially-developed elements. Most of the possibilities are already present, but some of them have to be recreated. The film will benefit enormously when certain extraneous and sometimes confusing elements have been eliminated.

When my study has been completed I will certainly meet with you, either here or in New York – when the dubbing has been completed. I, too, have a big stake in the final result and beyond that I have a responsibility as the Executive Head of this Corporation, which I cannot and will not ignore."

On October 21, 1962 I wrote a further letter to Mr. Mankiewicz in reply to a letter I received from him. I quote from my letter:

"Dear Joe. I returned from the Studio, after spending all of yesterday afternoon again screening the last act of CLEO, when I received your latest letter.

Originally in the projection room, in the presence of Dorothy Spencer and Elmo Williams, you completely agreed with my criticism of these physical elements.

You now state that the physical aspects are 'relatively unimportant.' I thoroughly agree with you – but we are 'stuck' with them. I didn't invent them or write them into the script. You and history did.

Although audiences would be disappointed and the critics would certainly howl, and history would be ignored, I wouldn't mind seeing all of these awkward, amateurish battle episodes eliminated. This is, of course, an impossibility, but this is where you have missed the point of my previous letters. I never expected the Battle of Actium to provide the equivalent of a BEN HUR chariot race. My complaint is that it is second-rate film making which fails to convey the disaster that befell Cleopatra and Antony.

Since we are compelled to show a battle and not just talk about it and push little toy boats around a table, it is vital that we attempt to pictorially represent it to audiences and not to rely on B picture devices. It is not a question of trying to introduce a 'physical thrill.' It is merely a question of finding a solution that will not affront or disappoint the public and the critics.

This episode serves a definite dramatic purpose in the story, and for that reason and that reason alone it must have distinction and size.

In presenting the Procession of Cleopatra into Rome, the camera had effectively and dramatically illustrated what I am talking about. The pomp, splendor and magnificence of the Procession is original and breathtaking. It is just exactly the opposite of the Battle of Actium.

As a matter of fact, in my opinion, with the exception of the Procession, there is not one physical episode in the film that has any size or dimension, or that properly conveys in pictorial terms what the players are continually talking about and 'describing.'

Everything gives the impression of being either 'off stage' or skimpy. The battles and conquests are talked about but never shown, and in some places not even indicated in dialogue.

Of course we need not show them all, but when we <u>are</u> forced to show something then we must show it in a comparable light with the balance of the picture.

The opening sequence of the film, on the battlefield with Caesar and Antony, is ridiculous. I have no feeling that a great battle has been fought and that thousands have been killed, and that Caesar has emerged as a triumphant victor. All I see is a lot of bonfires burning on the hillside in the background, and neither Caesar nor Antony give me any impression (except in dialogue) that they have been through a blood bath. Furthermore, I am unable to follow (even after repeatedly reading the script) exactly what they are talking about and why all the dramatic emphasis is put on the discussion of whether Brutus is to be killed or not. It seems to me that the main issue should be Caesar's decision to go to Egypt. We should learn the reason why, and perhaps Antony would take the opposite side and urge Caesar to return to Rome to receive his just rewards as a glorious hero – but Caesar is set on Egypt, and he sends Antony to Rome as his emissary.

I think we have got to emphasize with vigor the reasons why Caesar feels compelled to go to Egypt. At this point, Brutus is insignificant or secondary, and the same is true of Pompey.

I see this scene played on a battlefield drenched in blood. It is sunrise or sunset. Caesar should be surrounded by his staff, and we should see hundreds of prisoners being herded before him. The battlefield should be littered with dead as far as the eye can see. Riderless horses wander about in the background, as the line of prisoners goes by. I want to smell and feel blood, and I want our first opening shot in the picture to overwhelm an audience by its size, not simply from the standpoint of size but because I believe that this first sequence, if properly written and staged, will instantly impress audiences and help us in later sequences where, physically, we are 'skimpy.' If we overwhelm an audience at the beginning and take away the B picture look, we can later on in the story get by with episodes that are now talked about and not shown, or even with certain physical aspects which appear to have been undeveloped.

I would like to see both Caesar and Antony looking like soldiers. Perhaps even the first shot of Caesar against this panorama would be something simple like washing the sweat and blood off of himself, or having it done by his servant, as he grimly watches the procession of beaten prisoners go by.

When Antony arrives, I also visualize him looking like he has come out of a battle and a really bloody fight, and not just looking like a courier who rides in to deliver a message. You are introducing two of the three most dramatic historical characters in your film, and I think they come off second-rate. Behind it all I would like to see the victorious legions of Caesar. I would like to see their standards. I think this type of presentation has enormous values for the balance of the picture and, as I have said, its main point should be on the issue of why Caesar goes to Egypt.

It serves no point in telling me that you were prevented from doing certain things throughout the picture that you wanted to do. I have read three independent day-by-day production reports. The 'squeeze' came after you had spent more than 30 million dollars, and when there was very little money left to spend.

You were not deprived by the 'Administration' when it came to the Procession into Rome. It was not the fault of the 'Administration' (Heaven knows I have no desire to vindicate them) that you wrote the script during production (or at least re-wrote it). You had been on the project for many, many months prior to the commencement of photography. You knew long in advance of the written and signed commitments with Liz and others. The production was moved to Rome on your recommendation.

I am not going to ask you why the script was not completed prior to production, but it is only reasonable to point out that this caused you to shoot the major part of the picture in continuity.

Important actors waited weeks and months before ever appearing, and then they were carried on and on endlessly before they reappeared. This shooting in continuity resulted in at least 7½ million dollars of added production costs which do not appear 'on the screen.' Sets were built on overtime and then left idle for weeks and months. Some of the exteriors waited so long that they had to be repaired or reconstructed. Can this fairly and honestly be charged to 'Administration'? These are production decisions, and in this case they were not only vital but tragic.

Liz was ill a number of times, but the production reports shows that she was not 'called' more than 30% of the time, when you were concentrating on other episodes that did not involve her. Burton worked less than a week in the first 17 weeks he was in Rome. Roddy McDowall was called once in the first 4 months. I am only quoting samples, but these samples indicate why the picture now costs more than 33 million dollars.

You were not the official producer, yet in the history of motion pictures no one man has ever been given such authority. The records show that you made every single decision and that your word was law. You were never denied anything until the last 3 or 4 weeks of the picture, when the treasury had begun to sag and Moskowitz and the others arrived with the 'ultimatum.'

I cannot absolve Spyros of his share of responsibility. He was in a desperate personal situation, but since he was not a picture-maker, and since Peter Levathes had no production knowledge, and since both Doc Merman and Sid Rogell were either powerless to act or useless, you were indisputably in the driver's seat. On this point I do blame 'Administration' for giving any one man such unlimited authority. They did not give it to me on 'THE LONGEST DAY.' I had to fight for every inch of it.

Comparisons are always somewhat ridiculous, and the only motive I have on this point is to point out that the financial tragedy that has occurred cannot fairly or properly be placed on the head of Spyros or his subordinates. I am fully aware that you worked hard and devoted yourself to the project. No one can deny this. I am not interested in pin-pointing the blame on any individual, but certainly you cannot reasonably hold the 'Administration' responsible when you had the final decision and total control of when, how and where you shot.

In the opening paragraph of your letter you say that you have not yet finished the editing of the film. May I refer to your previous correspondence to me on this subject, and especially to your communication to the effect that the reason you wanted to do the dubbing on the selected dates was because you first wanted to complete your version of the editing. Again, I only mention this because you do.

In your second paragraph, you question 3 points: My 'possible extensive second unit operations' refers to the repair work and design of the Battle of Actium and to two other vital incidents that are referred to in dialogue and not even shown or indicated. One of them I consider indispensable. This is the rise of Mark Antony to power, prestige, glory and the idol of Rome. This can be done effectively and briefly, using ingredients, personnel and facilities that would also be used for the re-take I visualize for the opening sequence. Antony comes upon us now as a cardboard figure without anything but narration to indicate that he is ostensibly the 'new Caesar.'

'Important re-takes' refers to matters I have already discussed. 'Radical possibilities' refers to the March 1st date. I am already examining every conceivable possibility. Sketches for the miniatures of the Battle of Actium are already in the works at the Studio in Hollywood and in London, and the continuity of an under-

standable and legitimate 'battle plan' is being prepared
for this particular episode.

Referring to your comment about the 'types' of
material in which my touch is more gentle and understanding than in others, I have very little to say and
would prefer the record to speak for me. It has been a
varied record and I am not altogether ashamed of it.

Now let me set you straight once and for all.
With the exception of 3 episodes and part of a 4th episode, there is not one scene in the picture involving
Cleopatra and Caesar or Cleopatra and Antony that I
have anything but the highest praise for. I told you this
the first time I saw the film. I believed it then, and after
running the film again and studying it, I still subscribe
to it without qualification or hesitation.

I quarrel with many minor incidents within the
framework of these brilliant scenes, but I believe they
can be handled editorially. These basic key scenes between the three principal players, with the exceptions
noted above, have been written, directed and acted
magnificently.

My concern is basically with the continuity and
construction of the story. Once again, a great deal of
this could be rectified in the cutting room, but it calls
also for additional episodes to bridge the many bridges
that the story has to cross, and particularly the bridge
from the Caesar story to the Antony story.

In studying the film and the script, I find that a
number of eliminations have been made of bits of dialogue here and there that have important bearing on
characterization and continuity. I find the picture load-
ed with extraneous incidents and episodes which have
only secondary bearing on the story of Cleopatra and
Antony. In my opinion, these episodes add confusion,

and in some cases bring up issues that are better left unspoken.

We go into detail about enormous things that have only indirect bearing on the basic story line and, by the same token, we miss key moments or important information that we should have to more fully enjoy the basic story.

A rearrangement of the continuity and more or less drastic elimination of superfluous episodes will remove certain inexplicable events and place the dramatic emphasis where it belongs. Outside of normal 'tightening' I would not touch the fundamental key episodes between the three leading characters. Even when I don't clearly understand some of the things they are doing or saying, I am fascinated by them in almost every instance.

In your last paragraph you ask for an 'unequivocal statement' of where you stand in connection with the film. I will answer your question as bluntly as you have put it.

On completion of the dubbing, your official services will be terminated. If you are available and willing, I will call upon you to screen the re-edited version of the film. After you have done so, I will meet with you and go over it reel by reel and debate any points of difference that may arise. I will carefully consider any and all suggestions or objections that you may have to anything that has been done with which you disagree. I mean this sincerely and am prepared to take time to sit down with you reel by reel when then next version is ready. On the matter of re-takes or additional scenes involving principal actors, I will make every effort to obtain your services, if you are available."

I specifically call your attention to the last 3 paragraphs of the above letter. I clearly left the door open but retained the final authority as specified in Mr. Mankiewicz's employment contract. I stated my position clearly and I believe frankly. I do not have the authority to delegate "powers" that I do not possess. This is a Twentieth Century-Fox film, financed and owned by Twentieth Century-Fox Film Corporation.

When I arrive in New York I read in the press that Mr. Mankiewicz had announced that he had been "fired" and that he had been "arbitrarily dismissed." He made no reference whatever to the door I had left wide open to him. I have been around too long to be unnecessarily disturbed by irresponsible accusations and obnoxious publicity. Miss Elizabeth Taylor and Mr. Richard Burton were also quoted in the press, but <u>at that time</u> they were not aware of the correspondence that existed between Mr. Mankiewicz and me. Mr. Billy Wilder ran true to form. No experienced "Production Head" can ever expect sympathy in a publicized conflict with an "Artist." I am no exception.

Twentieth Century-Fox is a publicly owned Corporation with approximately 35,000 stockholders. As President I have a responsibility to the stockholders and I have an even greater responsibility to the hundreds of employees whose jobs have been terminated in a desperate effort on my part to perpetuate this Corporation and to eventually provide employment to the Studio personnel. I also have the responsibility of dealing fairly and honestly with "film-makers" whether they be producers, directors, writers or "artists." I cannot, nor will I, delegate this authority or duck this responsibility. I have liberally observed all of the terms of Mr.

Mankiewicz' contract and I have gone far beyond either the legal or moral issues involved.

Once again can I call your attention to the last 3 paragraphs on my letter to Mankiewicz dated October 21, 1962 which was my last communication to him. What I said then, I say now. What has been said otherwise, has been said to the press by Mr. Mankiewicz.

It is my considered opinion that Mr. Mankiewicz deliberately provoked this actually non-existent "conflict" for the purpose of shifting any future "blame" to me. If the film justifies its cost and is an enormous success than Mr. Mankiewicz as the director gets his full share of the credit. However, should the film not justify its unparalleled cost, then "Mr. Zanuck ruined it." I can find no other motivation for his action.

I have addressed this letter to you and the membership of the DGA in the interest of fair play. All of my correspondence "in full" is available for your inspection any time you see fit to examine it.

To avoid further distortion of the facts, I have bonded and sealed a black and white dupe print of the first cut of the film exactly as it was shown to me by Mr. Mankiewicz in Paris. This dupe print was taken off the original cutting print before the cutting print was sent to me in Paris. Together with affidavits by the film editor, Dorothy Spencer, and the head of the cutting department, Barbara McClean, this print has been deposited at Lyon Van & Storage Company under bond. This may appear to be an unnecessary or foolish precaution on my part, but since I have been subjected to baseless criticism, I want to be in a position to protect myself and this Corporation, and substantiate everything that I have said or written on the subject.

The bulldozers will not "raze the Studio" or plow it under, until I have exhausted every possible effort to restore the state of productive activity it once enjoyed, and until it is again employing a full complement of "film-makers" in every branch of the Industry, as well as providing rental facilities and equipment to "outside" producers like Wilder who is now leasing certain Studio equipment from the Fox lot to complete his current production.

To accomplish this for the benefit of the creative "artists" as well as for the hundreds of back lot employees, I need the support of everyone (guilds, unions and individuals) who are truly interested in preserving an important segment of this Industry.

Respectfully submitted,
Darryl F. Zanuck

Reception (1963)

1963: Jan 7

[Skouras to A. H. Howe, Vice-President of the Bank of America]

I am still optimistic about the future and there is no doubt in my mind that CLEOPATRA will prove to be the greatest of hits. As a matter of fact, I am confident that it will go even beyond our expectations.

Confidentially, we have already started to sell the picture on a hard-ticket policy, according to which we plan to open the picture in about 250 first-run theatres – all equipped with TODD-AO – in the most important cities in the world.

This should bring us approximately thirty-five million dollars front money from these theatres, together with a guarantee of about seventy-five millions.

Judging from the tremendous demand for this film from all over the world, we expect to receive in film rentals between $75,000,000 and $100,000,000 from these first-run theatres. I am quite certain that the future will justify my hopes and optimism.

1963: Jan 10

[Skouras to Tommy James]

... in the case of CLEOPATRA, which has cost us $40,000,000, it would be necessary for us to earn sufficient money in the beginning to recoup our negative cost. In order to recover our expenses we have to follow a hard-ticket policy in the beginning whereby we expect to get $35,000,000 front money and a guarantee of around $75,000,000.

1963: Mar 15

[Skouras to Tommy James]

... the sales on CLEOPATRA are terrific. Cash advances to date are already over $10,000,000. Nothing like this has ever happened before in the history of motion pictures. Therefore, there is no doubt in my mind that our goal will be reached and perhaps even surpassed.

1963: Apr 25

[Zanuck to Jerome Edwards]

Zanuck inquires about the book "The Cleopatra Papers." He writes that the manuscript "is now being offered to the top publishing firms by the literary agent, Ed Schulberg" and that Doubleday are "seriously considering it" but hesitate because of a $3 million lawsuit on another "celebrity" book. "Apparently, what [the authors] have done is ridiculed and crucified everything concerning CLEOPATRA and particularly the home office administration ... Outside of the home office personnel Mankiewicz emerges as the Great Villain. Nobody gets off easy except Walter Wanger is treated with sympathy." Zanuck is concerned that they might have had "access to a certain amount of correspondence" because they had been working in the publicity department under Charles Einfeld and had spent time in Rome. He questions the legality of employees publishing the company's correspondence and wonders if they had conceived the idea already during the production of "Cleopatra" and perhaps in coordination with Wanger ("The fact that they are sympathetic to Wanger is suspicious").

1963: May 23

[B. Duncan Boss to Skouras]
informs Skouras of the impending publication of "The Cleopatra Papers," excerpts from which would also appear in Esquire magazine. He also writes that excerpts from Wanger's book will appear on the June 1 issue of the Saturday Evening Post "with an additional printing of 125,000 copies."

1963: May

FOR IMMEDIATE RELEASE

SOFTCOVER BOOK SPLURGE ATTENDING PREMIERE OF FOX' "CLEOPATRA"

A record number of five softcover books, totaling 1,450,000 first-print copies, will be issued in conjunction with 20th Century-Fox's "Cleopatra," the Todd-AO spectacle which has its world premiere June 12 at New York's Rivoli Theatre.

Four of the five books will be titled "Cleopatra." The fifth is titled "My Life With Cleopatra," written by the film's producer, Walter Wanger, in collaboration with freelance writer Joe Hyams. Bantam Books, the publisher, has just brought it out with an initial print run of 500,000.

Bantam is also putting out a study of the Egyptian temptress by Emil Ludwig, for which the initial run

will be 200,000 copies. The three other Cleopatra
tomes are by Jeffrey K. Gardner (Pyramid), Carlo
Franzero (New American Library), and H. Rider Haggard (Pocketbooks). Their first print runs, respectively,
number 200,000, 250,000 and 300,000.

Franzero's work, originally published in Italy,
was a primary source for the screenplay, a collaboration
of director Joseph L. Mankiewicz, Sidney Buchman and
Ranald MacDougall.

"Cleopatra," starring Elizabeth Taylor, Richard
Burton and Rex Harrison, will premiere in more than
50 other U.S. and Canadian cities later in June.

1963: May 17

[Abraham L. Pomerantz to Bantam Books Inc.]
Gentlemen:

Our client, Mr. Spyros P. Skouras, tells us that
your imminent publication, "My Life With Cleopatra,"
by Walter Wanger and Joe Hyams is replete with crass
misstatements which reflect on Mr. Skouras' character,
integrity and executive ability.

I understand that the book is scheduled to be
published on June 9th. We demand that you cease and
desist from such publication and recall all copies that
may have been distributed. Otherwise we propose to
hold you liable for the very grievous and irreparable
damage you will do to the reputation which Mr.
Skouras has achieved over a long lifetime in the world
community.

I am sending you this letter by hand in the hope
of getting a prompt response.

Very truly yours,

1963: Jul 16

[Skouras' personal notes on "The Cleopatra Papers"]
INTRODUCTION TO "THE CLEOPATRA PA-
PERS"

The statement that the film was not getting
enough publicity and Brodsky was sent to Rome to supervise the American publicity at that end is not true.

It is customary for the Studio to assign a publicity man to any production on location.

The entire publicity and public relations on
CLEOPATRA were in the hands of GIULIO Ascarelli,
assisted by his 7-man staff. The Studio had sent Johnny
Campbell, but for some reason or other Walter Wanger
did not like him and wanted him replaced. Ascarelli reported this, urging that another man be sent, in order
to keep peace in the family.

When Peter Levathes went to Rome, without
advising anyone, he relieved Campbell of his duties in
Rome and assigned him to another picture, THE LI-
ON.

Then Charles Einfeld suggested that Jack Brodsky be sent from here. Personally, I did not want to
send anyone from here, preferring that the Studio send
a man from Hollywood. Finally, Brodsky was sent to
Rome as one of the group – not in charge of publicity.

NEW YORK, OCTOBER 18 [1961]

The statement contained in this letter is an honest one.
I was responsible for W. C. Michel, Executive Vice
President of Twentieth Century-Fox becoming president of the Executive Committee, to counteract and
eliminate the Operations Committee, of which Milton
Gould was chairman. It was my idea and my plan, and
it strengthened my position, instead of weakening it.

ROME, OCTOBER 20

The complaint was not that there was not enough publicity. The complaint was that it was not the proper kind of publicity. Much about the private lives of the stars, and not enough about the picture itself.

ROME, OCTOBER 28

This statement also is not according to the facts. He could not have known whether Mankiewicz made such a statement or not. As a matter of fact, I was the one who encouraged Mankiewicz to make the greatest picture of all time.

ROME, NOVEMBER 10

Again Brodsky speaks without knowing the true facts. One of the strongest points raised by both Mankiewicz and Wanger when they were pressing for the picture to be filmed in Rome was the six-day work week prevailing there.

NEW YORK, NOVEMBER 21

Weiss also speaks without knowing the true facts. According to the plan for promoting the distribution of the picture, it was decided to get a reel or two of the film to show to the exhibitors as a selling point.

NEW YORK, DECEMBER 26

[Skouras] had nothing to do with the building of the sets. They were designed by Mankiewicz and De Cuir.

New York, April 13 [1962]

The remarks about the testimonial dinner being "madness." These two men, who were being paid to create good will and good public relations, know very well deep down in their souls that this dinner was given to me not by any individual but by the whole industry getting together to honor me for the services I had rendered the industry over so many years. The statements which they make here are completely dishonest.

New York, April 17

I did not give any instructions to Nat Weiss. He was not of any importance. He was working for Mr. Einfeld and for Mr. Ascarelli. If I had given instructions for anything as important as "changing the public image," I would have given them to Mr. Wanger, or to Mr. Mankiewicz or to Mr. Ascarelli. This statement is not true. He never mentioned Liz Taylor to me or that I was nervous that he should not talk to her.

Rome, May 14

No one asked Mr. Wanger to send such a cable. He offered to do it. I never asked him to. The way it is presented here is completely untrue.

New York, May 28

Not true. I was in the hospital to be operated on and no one was acting "for" me or "because" I was laid up.

Phone call from Brodsky to Weiss, May 29

This is ridiculous. What did they know about the preparations? They assume an air of authority, as if they were playing an important part in the proceedings. Mr. Mankiewicz set the shooting date and he made all the "preparations" together with Walter Wanger.

Rome, June 7

Mr. Wanger was opposed to filming the battle of Pharsali and the battle of Phillipi. Mr. Mankiewicz and I were fighting for these two scenes. They would not have been filmed if it had not been for Mr. Zanuck taking over the production.

New York, June 16

"Newly-named" Fox Board chairman is certainly not correct. Judge Rosenman had been Chairman of the Board since February.

<u>New York, July 26</u>

Re: the Press Conference – this never happened. It was not necessary. If I had wanted to have a press conference I could have had it before, when the picture was completed.

<u>Rome, July 28</u>

The maudlin "fin du siecle" air re: the "passing" of the Skouras era – and the company itself! The remark that "they (Messrs. Mankiewicz & Wagner) and the stature of their works" would survive it all – inferring that neither Mr. Skouras nor the company would, although the very dinner in his honor that they earlier called "madness" was a tribute to him and to his having built up one of the great empires in the motion picture business since he became president of the company. Indeed, both CLEOPATRA and THE LONGEST DAY are testimonials to his having fought all those who opposed making these two films.

<u>Notes at end of article</u>

Here again – mis-statements. Mr. Wanger was not "fired." His salary was stopped because he did not have a contract any longer. I opposed this move as I felt it was not in the best interests of the company for the producer not to be able to complete the picture, particularly since there were only two or three weeks left to do it.

1963: Jul 23

[Nizer to Skouras]

My dear Spyros:

… I realize how deeply you have been hurt by the unjust vituperative attacks upon you. You have given a lifetime to establishing a reputation for goodness and achievement, which could be matched by few men. To be belabored by faithless employees [Wanger], who, after receiving huge compensation, try to exploit their association with the company for their profit, is outrageous. You may be sure that we will put our resources behind the effort to vindicate your position and I hope this gives you peace of mind.

My affectionate regards.

1963: Jul 24

SKOURAS ANNOUNCES
LIBEL ACTION AGAINST
WALTER WANGER

Spyros P. Skouras, Chairman of the Board of Directors of 20th Century-Fox Film Corporation, announced today that legal proceedings will be instituted against Walter Wanger, for libelous statements made about Skouras in Wanger's recently-published paperback book about the production of "Cleopatra."

Mr. Skouras stated that the libel action will be included in a counterclaim to be filed in a suit brought by Mr. Wanger against 20th Century-Fox, Darryl F. Zanuck, Earl Wilson and Skouras.

According to Mr. Skouras, the Wanger book is filled with inaccuracies, falsehoods and distortions, flatly contradicted by the record and contrary to Mr. Wanger's own statements in correspondence written during the production of "Cleopatra." Said Skouras: "Mr. Wanger's book contains a malicious and wholly groundless attack upon me as a film executive, and also as to my integrity and reputation as a man, and I have referred the matter to my attorney, Mr. Louis Nizer, for appropriate action."

1963: Jul 29

[Skouras to Nizer]

I would like you to know that I am very happy that you represent me in this action against a person [Wanger] who tried to ridicule me and belittle my character by such unjust and unfair accusation. I have absolute faith and confidence that you will establish the truth and vindicate my position.

1963: Jul 30

Wanger should be charged as a man who did not accept his responsibilities.

As a producer he demonstrated a reckless and wanton attitude, spending money lavishly, without any thought of economy. He was not interested in economy, but in how much more money the company would spend. He never showed the slightest appreciation of the value of the dollar.

For example, he requested from the Studio ...... people, as against ...... people used in the filming of Ben Hur.

He charges negligence on our part, and yet we gave every support and cooperation to him and money was always available to them.

He never showed any concern about the difficulties I was faced with and the criticism leveled against me by the Board of Directors.

He took no measures to discipline the stars, yet he demanded that we adopt drastic measures against them, which, if adopted, would have been detrimental not only to their reputation, but to the interest of the picture itself and our company as well.

However, if some measure which he had advocated were adopted, he criticised us for doing the very thing he had requested us to do.

He neglects to mention the many unnecessary delays created in the filming of the picture, which he, as a producer, could have or should have prevented.

1963: Aug 1

For Immediate Release

Spyros Skouras, Chairman of the Board of Twentieth Century-Fox Film Corporation, sued Walter Wanger today for libel, demanding $2,000,000 as compensatory damages and an additional sum for punitive damages. The suit was included in a counterclaim signed by his attorney, Louis Nizer, to Mr. Wanger's suit against Twentieth Century-Fox Film Corporation, Earl Wilson, Darryl F. Zanuck and Mr. Skouras in the United States District Court in Manhattan.

Mr. Skouras, in his counterclaim, stated that Mr. Wanger's book, "My Life With Cleopatra" contained "false, scandalous and defamatory matter" concerning Mr. Skouras. Mr. Skouras further stated that "Mr. Wanger acted with actual malice, without just cause and excuse, in wilfull and wanton disregard of the truth, and with the wilfull and malicious intent to injure [him] in his professional reputation as a motion picture executive," and mar "his excellent name and reputation and the esteem in which he has been held in the motion picture industry and by the general public throughout the world."

1963: Aug 1

UNITED STATES DISTRICT COURT FOR THE
SOUTHERN DISTRICT OF NEW YORK
WALTER WANGER, Plaintiff,
                    against
TWENTIETH CENTURY-FOX FILM CORPORA-
TION, EARL WILSON, SPYROS SKOURAS and
DARRYL F. ZANUCK, Defendants.

63 Civ. 1633
ANSWER, COUNTERCLAIM and DEMAND FOR
JURY TRIAL

Defendant SPYROS SKOURAS, by his attorneys,
PHILLIPS, NIZER, BENJAMIN, KRIM & BAL-
LON, for his answer to the allegations contained in the
Fourth Cause of Action of the complaint herein, alleges
as follows:
[…]
         14b. Defendant SKOURAS is Chairman of the
Board of Directors of Twentieth Century-Fox Film
Corporation, was formerly President of said Corporation, and for many years has enjoyed an outstanding
reputation in the motion picture industry as one of the
industry's leading executives.
         15. Defendant's professional career depends
not only upon his competence as a motion picture executive but upon the continuance of his said excellent
name and reputation and the esteem in which he has
been held in the motion picture industry and by the
general public throughout the world.
         16. In or about the month of June, 1963, plain-
tiff Walter Wanger, contriving with one Joe Hyams and
Bantam Books, Inc., wilfully and maliciously intending

to injure and defame defendant SKOURAS in his good
name and professional reputation, did maliciously, in-
tentionally and wilfully compose, deliver, publish, print
and widely circulate, and did cause to be printed, published and widely circulated through the mails, on
newsstands, in book stores and by other means of public exhibition and sales, in and about the City and State
of New York and throughout the United States and
elsewhere, false, scandalous and defamatory matter of
and concerning defendant SKOURAS and his personal
character and professional competence, contained in a
paper-back book entitled "My Life With Cleopatra" by
Walter Wanger and Joe Hyams [...]

17. By the words and language contained in said
publications [...] plaintiff Wanger meant and intended
to mean, and said publication was understood by read-
ers thereof and by the general public to mean, that defendant SKOURAS is incompetent and irresponsible as
a film executive, that he was responsible for executive
mismanagement respecting the production of the motion picture "Cleopatra," and that he is lacking in personal integrity as well as professional competence.

18. The statements about and innuendoes respecting defendant SKOURAS, his personal integrity
and professional competence as a motion picture executive contained in said publication, as hereinabove alleged, were and are wholly false and defamatory.

19. At the time of composing, publishing and
circulating, or causing to be composed, published and
circulated the said publication [...] plaintiff Wanger
knew that said publication and the statements and innuendoes therein concerning defendant SKOURAS, as
hereinabove alleged, were false and defamatory, and
plaintiff Wanger acted with actual malice, without just

cause and excuse, in wilful and wanton disregard of the truth, and with the wilful and malicious intent to injure defendant SKOURAS in his professional reputation as a motion picture executive. In consequence of the foregoing, defendant SKOURAS requests punitive as well as compensatory damages.

20. By reason of said libelous publication, defendant SKOURAS has been severely injured in his professional reputation, has been held up to public scorn and ridicule and has suffered great mental pain and anguish – all to his damage in the sum of $2,000,000.00

WHEREFOR defendant SKOURAS prays for judgment:

I. Dismissing plaintiff's complaint herein against this defendant.

II. Awarding this defendant the sum of $2,000,000.00 on his Counterclaim against plaintiff for compensatory damages and an additional sum for punitive damages.

III. Granting this defendant the costs and disbursements of this action.

IV. Granting this defendant such other and further relief as to the Court may seem just and proper.

DEMAND FOR TRIAL BY JURY

PLEASE TAKE NOTICE that defendant SKOURAS demands a trial by jury of the issues presented by defendant SKOURAS' Counterclaim and plaintiff's reply thereto.

PHILLIPS, NIZER, BENJAMIN, KRIM & BALLON

By LOUIS NIZER

Attorneys for Defendant SPYROS SKOURAS
1501 Broadway
New York 36, New York

1963: Aug 2

[Kenneth Winckles (London) to Skouras]

The Press reaction frankly has been mixed, but there is
no doubt that there is a considerable undercurrent of
disappointment with the picture. Frankly, Spyros, this is
my own personal reaction, but I would not tell it to anybody but you. I fear that in the long haul this is going
to produce an adverse word of mouth and inevitably
reflect badly on the future grosses. The tremendous interest in "Cleopatra" and all the trappings will un-
doubtedly carry it forward on a wave of interest in the
early stages, but I am concerned as to how long this
will last when word of mouth inevitably starts move-
ment. The reaction from the first night audience was
not dissimilar to that in New York, and the reluctance
by the guests to talk about the picture could, I think,
only lead to one conclusion.

1963: Aug 14

On Aug 14 1963 Skouras informed Zanuck that "we are
presently estimating a loss from theatrical production-
distribution of $8,100,000 in 1963." An amount that could end
up to $10 million.

1963: Aug 21

[Zanuck to Ralph Hetzel]

infuriated by a statement in Simon and Schuster's July 15 press release ("THE CLEOPATRA PAPERS ... is a portrait of the film industry caught in the act of being its own incredible self."), Zanuck sends a letter to the heads of film corporation and motion picture guilds suggesting that "appropriate action be taken"; in another letter he complains "there is no excuse whatever for Simon and Schuster to indict an entire industry in advertising an irresponsible book written by a couple of 'small fry' in the publicity organization."

1963: Aug 22

[Skouras to Zanuck]

Dear Darryl:

The personal favor I wanted to ask of you is that we meet with the mutual friend of whom we spoke over the phone.

Our suit against Walter Wanger has already been filed and I hope that within a week or ten days my suit against Weiss & Brodsky and Simon & Schuster and Peter Treves as conspirators, will be filled.

Therefore, I need a man like him, who is in good standing with the press, with Columnists and Commentators, in order to present me publicly as I am and offset the picture that Wanger, Weiss and Brodsky tried to paint of me in such vicious, disgusting and dishonest way.

Throughout the years during our long relationship any time you were in difficulties and you called on me, I did everything possible to be helpful.

Now, I am asking you to help secure the services of this man for me and I know you will do your utmost.

With kindest regards,
Sincerely,

1963: Aug 26

[Skouras to Percy Livingstone (London)]
Now, I would like to ask you a favor. I will appreciate it
very much if you will be kind enough to send some
flowers in my behalf to Dr. Moustafa Khalil, the Egyptian Minister of Communications, who is presently at
the London Clinic. Also, please contact him and find
out when will he be able to attend one of the CLEO-
PATRA performances, and how many tickets he would
need. Then please get the tickets to him and send the
entire bill to me.

1963: Aug 26

[Skouras to Winckles]
I have read the London press and I can understand
how the critics differed in their evaluation of the picture. This is quite normal, as personal tastes differ.
However, the word of mouth advertising seems to be
excellent and judging from the returns to date the picture will do tremendous business.

The same thing is happening in New York,
where also the critics differed, and everywhere else
where the picture opened. It seems that in spite of what
some people say, everybody wants to see this picture
and that pleases me very much.

... [The following list will] give you an idea of the phenomenal business of CLEOPATRA during the eight
weeks it has been playing in the various cities:

CITY	8 WEEKs ACCUMU-LATIVE GROSS ($)
Atlanta	196,275
Baltimore	142,884
Boston	283,506
Charlotte	64,505
Chicago	485,385
Cincinnati	127,213
Cleveland	174,912
Dallas	192,860
Denver	126,230
Detroit	261,326
Fort Worth	113,561
Houston	161,808
Indianapolis	127,367
Los Angeles	535,086
Louisville	112,095
Memphis	105,970
Miami	165,377
Milwaukee	114,260
Minneapolis	138,207
Philadelphia	289,079
Phoenix	101,491
Pittsburgh	212,787
Portland	130,233
Richmond	99,225
St. Louis	210,002
Salt Lake	126,377
San Antonio	90,990
San Diego	118,157
San Francisco	294,191
Washington	228,584
New York 10 weeks	$770,038

1963: Aug 29

[Winckles to Skouras]

Business at the moment remains magnificent.

1963: Sep 5

[Nizer to Skouras]

I believe the Cleopatra Papers libels you. You have a cause of action against the authors, the publishers, Simon and Schuster, and perhaps even against the character referred to as "The Boat" [Peter G. Treves].

Moreover, the authors (if they can be dignified by that name), as former employees of the Company have violated basic ethical considerations, in revealing (without the Company's agreement) alleged confidential matters learned during their paid employment. This is compounded disloyalty and reveals their lack of character. Simon and Schuster, too, might search their consciences. As an old friend of yours, Schuster knew the injustice he was doing you, but in the hope of making a fast dollar from an unworthy project, he ignored proper publishing standards as well as personal friendship.

The whole venture is inglorious. The book is obvious trash, from the sickening preface, which strikes a breathless tone, as if the history of the United Nations was about to be presented, to the four letter words which are supposed to titillate sales. Also the book is a fraud. No matter how the authors struggle to justify it, this is not their correspondence. They admit on Page VII "editing these letters ... to clarify and simplify" and on Page VIII that "the phone conversations contained here are reconstructions." But they have not edited out, or reconstructed out, obscene expressions. These, in the interest of "truth," have been spelled out and repeated, and one can almost see the saliva flowing from their mouths and the publishers.

The book promises to be sensational but is trite and boring. The authors have not even succeeded in their deliberate attempt at pruriency.

You have an additional right to be outraged. The two boys who wrote it were befriended by you. One of them wrote you a letter of gratitude. And now the stab in the back for a dollar.

[However, Nizer advises against a lawsuit because it would dignify the authors (perhaps even rekindle sales). His duty is to protect his client and gives an example "I have always blamed Oscar Wilde's lawyer for permitting him to bring an unwise suit." Still, if Skouras decides to proceed, he will offer advice and support to his new lawyer.]

1963: Sep 12

[B. Duncan Boss to Skouras]
Taking Nizer's side, tries to persuade Skouras not to file a lawsuit for "The Cleopatra Papers." After carefully reading the published book, he concluded that it was based on personal correspondence between the authors and "not official company communications." Moreover, most of the book seems to be a compilation of "anecdotes" already in circulation in gossip columns. However, the overall portrayal of the movie and Skouras is not negative. Indeed, the references to Skouras add up to a story: "Spyros P. Skouras, one of the great men in the industry … was engaged in a battle to save 20th-Century-Fox from being destroyed from both without and within the company; to satisfy the

stockholders of the company, and at the same time fight off a three-pronged attempt to destroy him, wreck the company, and establish a new management under the control of a man incapable of the responsibilities. A character known as The Boat [Peter G. Treves] turns out to be the villain, and a protégé of Skouras – Peter Levathes – appears to be willing to play Brutus in the drama that has all the tragedy of JULIUS CAESAR – with Skouras, being Caesar, and his Empire being 20th Century-Fox. We get the pathetic picture of a strong, dynamic personality in the motion picture industry – now physically tired and weak from pain and sickness, being hounded by ruthless characters out to ruin him, but still trying his best to get CLEOPATRA finished within a reasonable cost and in spite of Elizabeth Taylor and Richard Burton, whose childish antics were adding to the complications of the production of the motion picture. All through the book it is clearly indicated that CLEOPATRA, if ever finished, would be the greatest picture in the history of motion pictures. When Skouras resigns, thus preventing the villains from winning, it is a sad day for the authors of the book." He fears that such content could easily be used to the advantage of the authors. Moreover, from a legal standpoint, the book's sympathetic portrayal of Wanger could be used against Skouras' and the company's lawsuits against Wanger.

1963: Sep 23

[Skouras to Nizer; letter delivered by messenger on October 10]

Dear Louis:

I am deeply grateful to you for the time and thought you devoted to your letter of September 5th in reference to the advisability of my bringing a libel suit against Weiss and Brodsky, the authors of THE CLE-OPATRA PAPERS. Your detailed, very concise, warm and friendly letter is greatly appreciated and I send you my wholehearted thanks.

You have analyzed the problem with much care and deep insight, and I agree with you when you suggest that 20th Century-Fox should bring the suit. If this were to happen, it would fully satisfy me.

But should the company refuse to bring suit, then I intend to go ahead with my determination to prepare legal action, for something has to be done so that the truth is revealed. I am convinced that a suit must be brought against all concerned in what I strongly feel has been a conspiracy to hurt, humiliate and embarrass me. This would include the authors, whom you so aptly describe as "pipsqueaks," but also the publishers, Simon & Schuster, and the Boat [Peter G. Treves].

I am very sorry, believe me, Louis, when I disagree with your suggestion that I refrain from legal action. I respect your wisdom and knowledge of the intricacies of the courtroom, but in this case I cannot remain quiet. I sincerely hope you will be patient enough to hear my views and sentiments and reconsider representing me.

Throughout my life I have never sued any man. Many people have wronged me and done me injustice, but only money was involved and I never considered money as valuable as my name and reputation.

I have struggled against tremendous odds in order to achieve some measure of success. I had to suffer much and endure many hardships, but I always tried to uphold my name and the name of my family, so that my children and grandchildren would be proud of their heritage. It is not fitting now to take such humiliation and embarrassment as I am now suffering because of the publication of this book. The circulation may very well be limited, as you suggest, but the very people who know Spyros P. Skouras, and whose opinion I value highly, have read or are reading the book. This continues to place me in a most embarrassing position.

When men like Hollis Alpert of the "Saturday Review," Patrick Dennis of "The New York Times," Paine Knickerbocker of the "San Francisco Chronicle," Haskel Frankel of the New York "Herald Tribune," Dr. Frederick Shroyer of the Los Angeles "Herald-Examiner," Bob Thomas of the "Associated Press," and many other recognized authorities come out in praise of such a book, <u>it cannot be ignored</u>.

I have always cherished the importance of a good name. At one time I was guarantor for $7,500,000 and I could very easily have gone into bankruptcy in order to avoid the consequences. But I fulfilled my obligations – at my own expense, including interest and compound interest – because I wanted to leave a legacy to my children and grandchildren, the legacy of an honorable name and a good example.

I have rendered services to my adopted country with great devotion and enthusiasm and also my native land, and to many other countries when opportunity presented itself – England, France, Italy, and later Israel, from the time of the revolution and up to date, and the Middle East – for the purpose of doing good and helping all mankind.

And now these two boys – to whom I gave such personal attention and help, to further their careers, for many years, ever since they had joined our organisation – have aimed at what I hold most precious in life. They and their accomplices have published a book full of lies, trying to ridicule everything I hold sacred and to destroy my name.

For the sake of dishonest dollars, they do not hesitate to try to destroy people, characters and reputations. People may dismiss them contemptuously and laugh at them. But I remember that the whole world laughed and shrugged its shoulders at another pip-squeak by the name of Hitler, permitting him to become, under our very eyes, a monster who almost destroyed the whole world, killed over six millions helpless, innocent people and helped slaughter many other millions throughout the world.

So I cannot be satisfied with the fact that the authors of the book might be dismissed contemptuously and laughed at. Nor would I be satisfied with money from them. I want nothing material from the two pip-squeaks. What I want is the truth revealed, the truth which will show them up as dishonest and liars. From Simon and Schuster, however, and the Boat, I want damages and when I win, I will give the money to some charity. I don't want the money for myself.

Max Schuster and his associates have known me for years. Max is supposed to be my friend and has worked with me on many worthy causes. When he accepted this book for publication, he became as guilty as the Boat and Weiss and Brodsky, two ungrateful boys in whom I had taken a special interest since they joined the Company and tried to help them in their careers.

In spite of this personal interest in them and regardless of whether or not their positions were minor and they did not have access to any high level confidential data, they nevertheless disregarded this personal interest I had shown in them for a long time and betrayed their trust when they were supplied with high level confidential information, even clandestinely, by the Boat. They violated all the principles of the fraternity of advertising, publicity and public relations.

I firmly believe that neither Weiss nor Brodsky had any thought of writing their book until long after they returned to the United State and were influenced to do so. Otherwise, I cannot believe that Weiss would have written such a letter of gratitude to me, which he did; nor that Brodsky would have come to my office and personally thank me for all I did for him.

Although the book pretends to favor me in the beginning, as it moves along facts are distorted, important events are ridiculed – such as the testimonial dinner given me by the top men of the industry – and even the way I speak is wrongly presented for ridicule, and incidents are mentioned without all the known facts presented.

For example, Weiss mentions the sleeping incident in Rome, when I left the hospital in Paris to go to Rome for the sole purpose of viewing the new footage of CLEOPATRA. Against doctor's orders and in great physical discomfort, I had visited Europe with a group of executives to screen the three pictures in production there. After screening THE LONGEST DAY in Paris, I was rushed to the American Hospital for treatment. Next morning I left the hospital to attend a promotional meeting on THE LONGEST DAY, with Darryl Zanuck and the company executives. Then at noon, still in great pain, I made a hurried trip to Rome.

Weiss knew, but he does not mention it in the book, that the doctor in Paris had placed a temporary catheter in me, which another doctor in Rome had to change, giving me injections of sedatives to relieve the terrible pain I was suffering. Weiss ignores this completely and also the fact that he begged me at the time not to go to the projection room.

But I had to go, so that I could be completely informed as to the exact quality of the new scenes. Since I had already seen most of the picture at the end of March – at which time I had sent the most enthusiastic cables to all our general sales managers and advertising people throughout the world, with the news that this was truly the greatest picture ever produced – I felt that it was vital that I see the new footage.

As the doctor had warned me that the injections would put me to sleep, I asked Weiss to be sure to see to it that I was awakened – should I doze – when the new scenes were shown. I could not postpone the showing until the next day, for I had to fly immediately to London to screen NINE HOURS TO RAMA and then return to New York for the stockholders meeting to report on all three productions.

This is what I mean when I say that these characters twist and distort facts and eliminate areas of importance for the sole purpose of discrediting me.

Regarding The Boat [Peter G. Treves], I told you how the man had tried to threaten me, telling me that a lawsuit would be brought against me and it would be best for me to become the Chairman of the Board and Chief Executive Officer of the company, with Peter Levathes president in name only. The Boat and [Board member Milton] Gould were using Peter to gain control of the company for themselves. When I refused to fall in with their schemes and I told the Boat I was not in the least concerned about any lawsuit, and did not give a damn about his threats, he became furious and left.

You know also that since his group controls the "Saturday Evening Post," when that magazine published parts of the Walter Wanger book, they chose the portions which they felt would be most unfavorable to me.

As a stockholder, who had his own representative, Milton Gould, on the Board of Directors, the Boat had access to all important information which, they say in their book, he passed on to Weiss and Brodsky, using every means in his command to malign me and destroy my character.

The Boat could easily have told them how I fought to continue the production of CLEOPATRA when Gould wanted to stop production. Also Gould and some other Directors wanted to stop THE LONGEST DAY, or make it into a documentary film, just as they stopped THE GREATEST STORY EVER TOLD, THE CHAPMAN REPORT and THE DAYS OF WINE AND ROSES.

These miserable people do not mention the difficulties and the struggles I had to go through in order to have CLEOPATRA produced.

The Boat also inspired Walter Wanger to write his book against me, although he knew that I had tried to fight against Judge Rosenman's decision to dismiss Walter Wanger. The Boat knew that I was the only one who fought against the dismissal and that when Judge Rosenman came to the hospital, after my operation, to ask my approval, – after the Executive Committee had already approved Wanger's dismissal – I had told him that this would be a terrible mistake, especially since the picture would be completed in another four weeks. I even offered to pay out of my own pocket Wanger's salary for the remaining four weeks necessary to complete the picture.

I am not that big a man that I can overlook these malicious people who vilify me and ridicule everything decent about me and my life and my name.

Also in the book, incidents irrelevant to the subject of CLEOPATRA are injected to cheapen and make fun of me. For example, a letter written by Dick Brooks to Brodsky in Rome is quoted in a deliberate plan to use my accent as an object of ridicule.

I do not deny that I have a strong accent – for my voice is well known throughout the world – but I am sure that my English is much better than indicated, and I know that the accent described in the book is not mine. Anyone with even an elementary knowledge of language would recognize this as a mid-European accent, not Greek. No Greek would speak like that, since the sounds "th" – both hard and soft – are part of the Greek alphabet and present no difficulty to a Greek speaking person. Obviously, the only reason for introducing that letter was to ridicule me.

These are my views and sentiments. But there is still another point in favor of bringing suit against the conspirators responsible for the publication of THE CLEOPATRA PAPERS and, in my judgment, this is a very strong point:

When we go to court with the Wanger suit, our case may be seriously jeopardized, if we don't do something about this other book. Wanger's lawyers surely will try to use this second book to his advantage, since in their book Brodsky and Weiss continually praise Wanger as a wonderful man and great motion picture producer.

These are my thoughts, Louis, and I beg you to forgive me for taking so much of your time with this letter. But I cannot accept this book without fighting for what I believe is morally right. The authors should publicly apologize to me for the wrong they have done to me.

I cannot accomplish this alone or without legal help. I need your skill, your ability – but more than that, I need your friendship and understanding – to present the truth and remove the stigma which this book attempts to place on my name.

I shall wait anxiously for your answer and I send you best wishes and warmest personal regards.

Sincerely,

Since writing the above, something rather extraordinary happened, which I would like to tell you about and which will show you to what extent this book has maligned my reputation.

The other night I attended a cocktail party given by Mrs. Golda Meir, the Foreign Minister of Israel, and I met many old friends there. Two or three mentioned this book to me and expressed their sympathy. Mrs. Max Schuster was also present and she came to me and told me she wanted to apologize to me for her husband. She felt that what was done to me was unfair and she wanted me to talk to her husband about it when he would join us in a few seconds. I thanked her very much, but walked away. I do not think Mr. Schuster saw me.

She also told me her husband had seen my lawyer, Otto Koegel, last week at the [New York] Philharmonic opening and she said he told her he had expressed to Mr. Koegel how badly he felt and admitted that he had made a terrible mistake. Otto himself told me this later and he also said Max was concerned as to whether I would sue or not and Koegel told him I was planning to do so. Otto said they spoke for a very long time about this subject and that Mrs. Schuster told them, in Max Schuster's presence, that her husband should not have allowed Simon and Schuster to publish such trash, particularly since it was against his friend, and that I did not deserve such treatment.

I have no hatred, enmity or vindictiveness in my heart against anyone, but I feel I must do something about this for the sake of my reputation and because if there is no attempt on my part to deny or oppose it, it would not be fair to my family.

If the company brings the suit, it will be in the best interests of all concerned, and the company has sufficient causes to take this action, if not for other reason, as a protective measure against Walter Wanger's suit.

I just received a letter from Otto Koegel and am attaching copy hereto as it concerns the above.

1963: Oct 2

[Koegel to Skouras]

Dear Spyros:

I was seated at supper after the Philharmonic benefit last week beside Mrs. Max Schuster (Ray), and two places distant from Max. It was inevitable that anyone dining with me, knowing of our relationship for a third of a century, would inquire about you.

The small talk soon led to a discussion of the "book" by Mrs. Schuster, who stated in Max's hearing that she had hoped the book would not have been published, that you were so sweet, etc. etc. Max, again and again enjoined me to tell you that he still loves you. As to the book, he said that if his firm had not published it, another surely would have. Repeatedly and quite earnestly, Max wished me to assure him that I would inform you of his continued affection for you.

Sincerely,

1963: Nov 14

[Albert F. Smith to Skouras]

Re: Wanger v. Twentieth Century-Fox, et al

Dear Mr. Skouras:

I enclose herewith a copy of the amended pleading which has been filed on your behalf in the Wanger case.

As you will note, we have now set forth ... the full text of those paragraphs from Wanger's book which are alleged to be libelous.

May I suggest that you review these pages preliminary to our preparation for your examination before trial, which will take place within the next few weeks.

Kindest personal regards.

Sincerely,

1963: Dec 2

[Koegel to Skouras]

Dear Spyros:

Walter Wanger in his so-called diary, under date of November 14, 1960 ... records the following:

"The insurance company offered Skouras $1,750,000 and promised to reinsure Elizabeth. He

wants more. The offer was presented by David Metcalf
who was one of the junior partners in the firm that carried our insurance ..."

I had a talk with David Metcalfe of Stewart,
Smith & Co., Limited about this. He agreed with me
that there was at no time an offer of the insurers to pay
us $1,750,000 and continue insurance on Miss Taylor.

1964: Mar 16

[Herbert C. Earnshaw to Frank H. Ferguson]
Re: Walter Wanger v. Twentieth Century-Fox Film
Corporation.

We had another half-day session of Mr.
Skouras' deposition in the above case. It was primarily
concerned with interrogation respecting all of the various contract documents. Mr. Skouras did extremely
well in handling more of the rather complicated problems which I am sure you are familiar with.

Walter Wanger was present during the course
of the deposition.

One of the more enjoyable points during the
afternoon arose when Mr. Skouras' testimony jarred
Walter Wanger to the very bottom of his high button
shoes. As you know, Wanger has always taken the credit as the sole creator of the idea to produce a motion
picture entitles Cleopatra and that he is the solely responsible for it. Mr. Skouras said, in effect, that Twentieth Century-Fox was considering making Cleopatra
long before Walter Wanger entered the picture. Mr.
Skouras said he recalled that it had been publicly so announced, he believed by Studio Press Release.

We have been requested to produce any such
press release or trade paper announcements.

[...]

I am enclosing a copy of the memorandum which David Brown prepared for Mr. Buddy Adler on April 25, 1960 which was among the papers which you sent me. It gives some of the history of Cleopatra.

1965: Aug 12

STATEMENT PROPOSED BY MR. NIZER

Walter Wanger, producer of the film CLEO-PATRA, today announced a full retraction of all statements and inferences in his book "My Life with Cleopatra" and in a condensed version of the book published in the Saturday Evening Post, which reflect adversely upon the personal integrity or professional reputation of Spyros P. Skouras, Chairman of the Board and former President of Twentieth Century-Fox Film Corporation.

Mr. Wanger stated that he is now convinced, upon reviewing all the evidence, including many internal documents from the Fox files, made available to him since his book was written, that he was mistaken in criticising Mr. Skouras' actions in connection with the production of CLEOPATRA.

Mr. Wanger's statement continues: "In all candor, I want to apologize to Spyros Skouras for the grave injustice done to him in my book and magazine article, "My Life With Cleopatra." I withdraw any statement or inference in the book and in the article which in any way accuses Mr. Skouras of mismanagement while he was President of Fox. I hold Mr. Skouras in the highest regard both personally and professionally, and deeply regret that anything I have written cast a cloud over the outstanding reputation of one of the acknowledged leaders and pioneer executives of the motion picture industry.

1965: Aug 12

STATEMENT PROPOSED BY MORRIS ABRAM

Spyros Skouras, Chairman of the Board of Twentieth Century-Fox Film Corporation, and Walter Wanger, producer of the film CLEOPATRA, today announced the amicable settlement of litigation between them, arising out of the production of that film.

Mr. Wanger stated that he withdrew any statements in his book "My Life With Cleopatra" and in a condensed version of the book published by the Saturday Evening Post, which might have been construed as reflecting adversely upon the personal integrity or professional reputation of Mr. Skouras, who at the time, was the President of Twentieth Century-Fox Film Corporation.

Mr. Wanger added that he was sure that Mr. Skouras' actions in connection with the production of CLEOPATRA were taken in good faith, and that he regrets any material in the book which could be interpreted as criticising Mr. Skouras' actions.

Mr. Wanger pointed out that every artistic production creates tensions and even misunderstanding. As CLEOPATRA was the largest motion picture production in history these circumstances were bound to be magnified in proportion to the size of the production.

Mr. Wanger's statement continues: "Mr. Skouras and I have been friends for many years, and I want to make it clear that I hold Mr. Skouras in the highest regard both personally and professionally, and would regret deeply if anything I have written inadvertently cast a cloud over Mr. Skouras' outstanding reputation when he was the President of Fox or at any other time."

Mr. Skouras stated that he welcomed Mr. Wanger's statements; that he is delighted that the faith he had in the film CLEOPATRA, produced by Mr. Wanger, has been justified by the praise which the film has received and its audience reception and financial success.

1965: Oct 14

FOR GENERAL RELEASE.

Spyros P. Skouras, Chairman of the Board and former President of 20th Century-Fox Film Corporation, and Walter Wanger, producer of the film "Cleopatra" today announced a discontinuance of Mr. Skouras' libel action concerning Mr. Wanger's book "My Life With Cleopatra."

Mr. Wanger announced that he withdrew all statements in his book "My Life With Cleopatra," and in a condensed version of that book published in the Saturday Evening Post, which reflect adversely on the personal integrity or professional reputation of Mr. Skouras.

Mr. Wanger's statement continues, "I want to express my deep regret to Mr. Skouras that anything I have written in my book and magazine article entitled "My Life With Cleopatra" has done him any injustice and I withdraw any such statement as I hold Mr. Skouras in the highest regard both personally and professionally. I regret that anything I have written has cast a cloud over his outstanding reputation as one of the acknowledged leaders and pioneer executives of the motion picture industry."

APPROVED

October 14, 1965

Walter F. Wanger

Skouras' interview on *Cleopatra* (1963)

1963: Mar 11

INTERVIEW BETWEEN DAVID SLAVIT AND SPYROS SKOURAS

SLAVIT: I am wondering, or part of my investigations have led me to wonder, how it was that $40,000,000 or so got spent on a movie and I was wondering whether one report that I heard has any substance or basis in fact, that is: One report has it that most of the reason for the extravagant cost of the picture was that sets were built before the script was finished – everything went ahead, sets were built at overtime then left idle. Wanger and Mamoulian both wanted to delay shooting for some weeks, or months, and the reason for all of this hurry has been attributed to you. You have Wanger and Mamoulian Carte Blanche, you were most anxious to have the picture in the can and on your desk before the June stockholder's meeting of last year, which might have avoided all of the difficulties that happened at the stockholders meeting.

SKOURAS: Who made that statement to you?

SLAVIT: Let's see if I can remember … I really can't tell without looking at my note books. I have been …

SKOURAS: This is very important part of your research and you must be able to remember how this came about. If you don't want to tell me, I will …

SLAVIT: One of three people, and it was only one of them. I came from an engagement straight here and have not prepared all these questions, and I have two desks almost that size, covered with notes, clippings and things about "Cleopatra." It was somebody who was with Fox and was fired and is not very happy about the whole thing.

SKOURAS: Tell me the three people – it will help me to give you the information you are seeking if you are looking for an honest record, or rather just a scandalous record.

SLAVIT: In confidence, it was either Brodsky, Weiss or Levathes – I don't think the latter because he spoke well of you.

SKOURAS: Brodsky or Weiss? They did not know anything about it. They were completely ignorant.

SLAVIT: There is no question that there was a good deal on [?] – whether it was because there was some reluctance to spend extra money ... I know Wanger asked Fox at one time to pay Elizabeth Taylor $1,000,000 extra and put off the whole thing until Spring.

SKOURAS: That never happened. If you want to know the facts, I would like to tell you. "Cleopatra" was conceived by Buddy Adler when he was the head of the Studio. Then, about the same time, Walter Wanger had announced that he was working also on "Cleopatra." I respected highly Mr. Wanger's showmanship, but I had greater confidence – I won't say greater – but I was more loyal to Mr. Adler since he was the head of the Studio. Mr. Wanger's agent, Charles Feldman, approached us to engage Wanger and we later engaged the British writer, Nigel Balchin to prepare the script. At that time, the budget was around $2,500,000 and Walter Wanger was attempting to build up the substance to a much more important production than we had in mind. We engaged Rouben Mamoulian as director.

SLAVIT: Who were some of the directors Walter Wanger refused before accepting Mamoulian?

SKOURAS: I had nothing to do with the Studio – Mr. Adler was head – any suggestions came by Mr. Adler. Walter Wanger was working directly for Mr. Adler ...

SLAVIT: Were you consulted at that time as to who should be the star? I understand Adler was interested either in Joan Collins or Dana Wynter.

SKOURAS: No, Adler was noncommittal – he always wanted Elizabeth Taylor. I tried to convince him, without con[?] but he didn't come out with it, he never favored anybody, and I suggested Joanne Woodward, Sophia Loren and Gina Lollobrigida.

SLAVIT: Who thought of Susan Hayward?

SKOURAS: Walter Wanger, as far as I remember.

SLAVIT: It sounds reasonable.

SKOURAS: Joanne Woodward, I suggested to Adler, would give a tremendous performance, but none of these stars appealed to him. One day he told me he would like to work with, engage Elizabeth Taylor. I am trying to tell you as accurately as I can remember. So, the first man who talked to me about Elizabeth Taylor was Buddy Adler. How it came about because of her great [performance] in "Cat On A Hot Tin Roof," Walter Wanger or Lou Schreiber, or her agent, Kurt Frings – I don't know how, but Buddy Adler called me up and told me that she agreed to play the part, provided we agreed to produce the subject overseas.

SLAVIT: Are you sure that this is true? Because Miss Taylor denied this in a cable to me this morning.

SKOURAS: I can verify the subject by contract. I don't know whether Elizabeth Taylor opposed this – I am not in this position because I did not participate in negotiations. I am telling you the way I know the story. When Adler told me this, I became frightened because I always was afraid of overseas productions. I opposed it as much as possible, because of and experience I have had from time to time, but Buddy insisted. I opposed two things – the overseas production and the very high salaries. It was then over $1,000,000.

We were to produce the picture in London with exteriors in Rome and to do the film before "Butter-field-8." The M-G-M people, however, pre-empted their rights to her, so the negotiations collapsed and we started looking for other personalities and we had many talks with Gina Lollobrigida and Mamoulian and Wanger, and took tests of many girls – I don't know how many. Then again, the negotiations with Elizabeth Taylor were re-opened. I was greatly pleased when Buddy Adler told me that he received the script and everybody seemed to be satisfied and happy. Then Elizabeth Taylor was ready to go overseas to Rome – she attended the Olympic Games, and then went to Greece and from there to London and they had pre-pared the sets in London and the costumes and they were ready to start sometime in October. With the exception of two or three appearances for tests, Elizabeth was never really photographed in any scene. It was so unfortunate that her illness was much more serious than the doctors disclosed and they advised us from time to time. We had difficulties with the Insurance Companies and the Insurance people strongly recommended to us to shoot around her, which Mamoulian agreed to do. He did a great deal of shooting and then Mr. Adler advised that he did not like the script. He sent the script to me to read. Then we heard many stories that there was a great deal of disagreement between Walter Wanger and Mamoulian about the script.

SLAVIT: Which one of them did not like the script?

SKOURAS: Well, the complaints came first from the Studio, from Mr. Adler, and there was a great deal of commotion. Buddy Adler died before shooting for the picture started.

SLAVIT: He died before shooting started in England.

SKOURAS: He complained about the script – he was the first man to show dissatisfaction.

Bob Goldstein succeeded Buddy Adler. Sidney Rogell was signed to act as the production manager, not from the creative point of view, but from the physical point of view and he became involved between these two men and the script.

SLAVIT: May I ask you a few questions?

SKOURAS: Let me tell you the whole story, then ask me the questions – I am gathering my memory.

They decided to have a new writer and it was suggested in the Studio at a meeting between Bob Goldstein, Joe Moskowitz and Charlie Feldman, who represented both Wanger and Mamoulian. So we asked Nunnally Johnson to step in and we called up Walter Wanger and they all agreed to it. However, Mamoulian opposed Mr. Johnson's conception. Johnson worked very hard and I am sure he would have written a wonderful script, but it seems Mamoulian by this time be-

came very close friends with Elizabeth Taylor and Mamoulian complained that he could not make the script
changes that Nunnally suggested, because it was already
finished and was approved and Rogell thought that it
was too much waste of time. By this time, Elizabeth's
health improved, although she was still sick and, when
Mr. Rogell gave a date for Mamoulian to start the picture, he sent me a telegram resigning. This was to the
great satisfaction of Walter Wanger and Rogell, and
they asked me to contact Joe Mankiewicz. Charles
Feldman, who also represented Mankiewicz, came to
New York and we accepted Mamoulian's resignation
and Mr. Moskowitz engaged Sidney Buchman to write
his story concept. Mankiewicz had good understanding
of the subject and had already given a fine treatment of
the story. By this time, Elizabeth was well, but they
were not ready to shoot. They were prepared to shoot
within a few days and she got sick again and almost lost
her life. When she was sick, I was asked by many of the
people, like you in particular, and the English press,
"why don't hire some other star?" And I said, "Elizabeth Taylor is Cleopatra," and I acclaimed her as the
only artist who could play the part. Then, when she was
violently sick again, many other artists offered their
services, but I took the decision that only Elizabeth
Taylor could play the part. I believe that my judgment
added a great deal of credulity to the subject. My confidence in Elizabeth gave great standing to "Cleopatra" –
it made "Cleopatra" a news topic in every place in the
world – in South Africa, India, Japan – everyone talked
about it. Even in Greece they talked about "Cleopatra."

Mankiewicz worked very devotedly on the subject and engaged MacDougall. MacDougall wrote a
wonderful script. You can imagine the different ver-

sions from brilliant people each time ... not from ordinary writers. MacDougall did a great job and it is true that Mr. Joe Mankiewicz did a magnificent job in writing wonderful, wonderful dialogue, but the story and the script was there – he changed very few scenes so far as I know ... but his dialogue gave the story a great deal of prominence – gave it true substance. The whole world will cherish the magnificent dialogue of these three people, particularly.

I was relieved, in spite of the $6,000,000 cost, that the picture was going to be produced in Los Angeles. Joe insisted the picture must be produced overseas. He felt it was necessary to make the picture in Rome and Egypt to get the right atmosphere. All of us opposed it. Everyone in the Company became frightened. The Studio people approached us at that time – they were convinced in some way that the cost would be substantially increased if the picture was produced overseas.

Elizabeth Taylor's doctor at that time was Rex Kennamer. He called me up and he told me they were trying to get him to agree to prompt Elizabeth Taylor to go overseas and he asked my advice and I said that would be suicide. She had a contract giving her the right to make the picture overseas. The man who will give you more light on this subject, as to how it happened, is the lawyer, Martin Gang. He represented her. So, Dr. Kennamer came to see me two or three times – he says if the girl has good health to make the film in the US, she will be just as well in Rome or Egypt. The manager of the Studio, Doc Merman, favored making the picture overseas. The reason was because we had a number of productions and also "The Greatest Story Ever Told." The lawyers got together and insisted on the star's rights. The doctor assured us she would be in good health and we had no alternative if we wanted Elizabeth Taylor. By this time, I had built her up as "Cleopatra," so we asked Joe Mankiewicz and Walter Wanger when we could start the picture. There never was any question that they would not be ready to start the picture. In the meantime, this was the early part of summer. Joe made a trip overseas.

When we went to Europe, we made mistakes – we did not make a European picture, we made an American picture in Europe. Mr. Mankiewicz and Walter Wanger asked for 90 technicians to proceed to Rome. They did an amazing job in making some of the greatest scenes anybody could see in any film – amazing splendor – really you feel that a great Queen enters into ancient Rome ... I never saw such a scene in my life. Unfortunately, the weather got bad and it took three or four more days to finish the exteriors. This bad weather break was very costly. Thousands of people were engaged – all the technicians had to be kept there for a few weeks until the weather got better again. I, as president of the Company, assumed all responsibility. I could not blame anybody because these people were authorized, but if they feel I am to blame for it, I accept the blame. But I assure you it was not my doing that the picture turned out to be so costly ... I entrusted people to do the job – I was not making the picture, other people were making it. I admire the picture they made, but am naturally disappointed at the cost.

The date was set by Joe Mankiewicz, Walter Wanger and his lawyer at the Coast and I was not there when the date was set.

SLAVIT: Didn't they know?

SKOURAS: They didn't expect the weather. They lost about a week or ten days in their preparations. This is probably the most expensive picture of all times and I think this is going to be the greatest picture that was ever produced.

I was so happy when Mr. Zanuck became president and associated himself with "Cleopatra." You can imagine the cost had greatly plagued me, and I had to accept the responsibility, Dave. I could not say to the other people it was not my fault.

Mr. Zanuck, to my delight, agreed with both Joe Mankiewicz and myself that the battles of Pharsalia and Philippi should be photographed. Wanger did not favor it. They tried to interfere when the cost of the picture got high, but I thought the battle of Pharsalia was so vital and important.

SLAVIT: Was it Wanger or Bob Goldstein who interfered?

SKOURAS: These parts had been shot long before. The battle of Pharsalia was important because it is here that Julius Caesar defeats Pompeii … that is how he met Cleopatra. Darryl knew nothing about it. Some other people opposed it, and thank God, when talking to me about it, said "put in these two scenes, the battles of Pharsalia and Philippi."

Never before in history has any picture been handled so dramatically from the distribution point of view. Records were broken in publicity and there has been tremendous word-of-mouth. Also, records have been broken in the salesmanship. Seymour Poe and Joe Sugar have planned to re-coup a good part of the cost of the picture before it opens.

SLAVIT: You don't pay interest to the exhibitors, but you were paying interest to the bank.

SKOURAS: With all the responsibility and the blame, I must assume some of the credit with Seymour and Joe, because I think we are going to get, I am confident we will get, a substantial amount before the film will start playing. This is my story. Now ask the questions.

SLAVIT: In the story you recounted, you mention several different script writers involved in the picture. From what I understand, Laurence Durrell was engaged by Mankiewicz who later agreed Durrell was not a script writer.

SKOURAS: I don't think Mankiewicz engaged Durrell – it was after Nigel Balchin that Durrell was engaged, but I don't remember if Durrell was engaged by Joe Mankiewicz … maybe he talked to him, but he engaged Sidney Buchman. Joe was working favorably, and I don't remember the instance as well as I remember that Durrell was engaged by Mamoulian and Walter Wanger.

SLAVIT: Walter Wanger told me and showed me that this is included in the manuscript of his book, which will be "My Life with Cleopatra," to be published in June. He said that before shooting in England started, there was a meeting of the Board of Directors of Fox when it was decided that Walter Wanger was to be the producer, but that all authority and decisions were to be made by Bob Goldstein and in case of any disputes between the two, Buddy Adler would make the final decision. Do you remember any such meeting?

SKOURAS: First, I don't remember Walter Wanger ever being in a Board of Directors meeting.

SLAVIT: Words to the effect that he read it in some minutes.

SKOURAS: Buddy Adler decided to go to Europe. This European trip was responsible for his death, there he got a virus. He was starting to improve but he came down with double pneumonia. He became so enthused by the great possibilities of "Cleopatra" in Europe and he felt a most spectacular film would be made in Rome. It was his decision while he was in London to make the picture in Todd-AO. He appointed Bob Goldstein to represent him in London while he was at the Studio, but Walter Wanger was the producer and Mamoulian was the director. You have to know Walter Wanger well – he is a fine man, but he likes to have lots of people to help him. Off the record, he does not want to work so hard. I paid the penalty, but I am confident that "Cleopatra" will pay good benefits and I am so happy Mr. Zanuck is associated with the picture.

SLAVIT: Walter Wanger also says …

SKOURAS: I would prefer not to – you have to know Walter Wanger – if you know him, then you can put credulance in his statements.

SLAVIT: I want to know how much credulance, which is why I have to ask this question.

SKOURAS: It is for you to make the decision regarding Walter Wanger's statement – it is up to you.

SLAVIT: Is it true that when you hired Mankiewicz to take the place of Mamoulian, who resigned, you wanted to fire Wanger? That you retained Wanger only at Mankiewicz's insistence and that Wanger knew that?

SKOURAS: There is no question of that. I didn't want to fire Wanger. I was worried about Wanger and I wired Joe Mankiewicz to take full responsibility. He has tremendous confidence in Walter Wanger … we paid a lot of money to Joe – I was buying a director-producer, not the director, but it is true that Joe wanted Walter Wanger to remain.

SLAVIT: I understand from Mr. Mamoulian that he was first sent to Rome to look at sets there. Then the picture was going to be shot in Hollywood, then England with exteriors in Rome, then it was decided that the entire picture should be shot in England with the exteriors in England, and I have never been able to find out whose decision that was. Mamoulian says he told you that this was a crazy idea and that you told him "I am president of the Company, and it is up to me to make the decision" and he said, "Yes, but you are wrong."

SKOURAS: This is not true. This decision came by virtue of the following:

As a British quota film, we had to transfer location, British technicians, cameramen and artists so the cost would be fantastic at that time – $2,000,000 or $3,000,000. The decision was not made by me; the decision was made by Buddy Adler and Bob Goldstein and the production department. As a matter of fact, the poor man (Adler) was at the Cedars of Lebanon Hospital when he made the decision that we would not go to Rome. It would have cost terrific sums of money. We had to move all the people from London to qualify for the Eady plan. This was a production decision. The distribution department and everybody felt it would be a terrible mistake not to make it on an Eady Plan picture.

SLAVIT: Is there any truth in the report I hear that one of the reasons that the decision was made in the first place to shoot an Eady Plan picture in England was because Goldstein was head of European production and there was no production in Europe.

SKOURAS: No. Let me reconstruct the events. Mamoulian went to Rome. Buddy Adler engaged a man, Santi, to be co-producer and Mr. Mamoulian was not impressed by Santi's production staff. Mamoulian is a very high class artist and worked on productions such as "Oklahoma," "The King and I," and "Carousel." He wanted to make a really fine motion picture and he appealed to us to move away from Rome and go to London, but he wanted Rome as a location. When the Eady Plan was approved, the British Government said we could not very well withdraw our agreement ... Wanger and Mankiewicz told me Goldstein was not crazy about it.

SLAVIT: In Elizabeth Taylor's first contract, there was a clause saying that the production must be overseas. Could I see this contract?

SKOURAS: The lawyers have it. You can take my word – nobody would ever oppose it because it is a reality and the organization made the contract with Elizabeth Taylor.

SLAVIT: Do you remember the name of her Swiss Corp? After that first episode with Mamoulian, there was for a time talk of doing the picture with Mankiewicz in Hollywood. All the costumes were shipped from Pinewood.

SKOURAS: I thanked God that we were going to make the picture in our own Studio. There was no question but Joe opposed it ... he was responsible for altering the opinion of everybody because he felt it would be the best picture from the artistic point of view and cost less money ...

SLAVIT: You also mention that one of the things that bore on this decision was the squeeze in space at the Fox lot.

SKOURAS: Doc Merman wanted the picture to go to Rome. Levathes asked me to come to the Studio and talk to George Stevens and he delayed shooting "The Greatest Story" for about six months. He gave some of his people to Mankiewicz. Eddie Fisher did not want the picture to go overseas, but Martin Gang went along because of the benefits for Elizabeth Taylor.

SKOURAS: Merman's objection to studio shooting was that you had "The Greatest Story" plus Levathes' television productions and that the Company could not afford both "The Greatest Story" and "Cleopatra" at the same time. Is this right? Also, that the television networks did not renew some of the programs?

SKOURAS: Well, many miscalculations like that took place. "The Greatest Story" had nothing to do with "Cleopatra." It was decided by production to go to Rome. I felt I had to step out … I had too much at stake; after all, I am the largest stockholder in the Company – I was at that time and still am today and many of my friends have blocks of stock in this country because of me. Mr. Zanuck is a big stockholder … Mr. Zanuck and myself are the largest stockholders, then Harry Brandt.

SLAVIT: In the decision to go to Rome, one thing puzzles me …

SKOURAS: What are you trying to find out? What is your purpose? I took you in my confidence and told you the whole story and you know that it was not contrived at all. What is your aim? Here is the greatest picture property that was ever produced … in choosing a subject of such great, historical value. I can assure you that Joe Mankiewicz did a magnificent job in directing it. It will be of tremendous importance to family life because it deals with historical interest.

SLAVIT: I am trying to find out how it all happened. I think it would be naive of me to say here is a picture costing $40,000,000, of which $20,000,000 was spent by accident ... Mr. Skouras spent $20,000,000 by accident. It didn't happen that way ... part of it was bad luck, accidents, weather, illness, etc., which could not have been avoided.

SKOURAS: Here is my worry ... I find the film cost at least $20,000,000 more than it should have cost. There were many conditions which brought this about. I did not give Carte Blanche to Mankiewicz, but I gave him full authority creatively. We had people like Sid Rogell and Walter Wanger and all these people were there to see the job was done in the most economical way and meeting the requirements of the director.

Human beings away from home make a lot of mistakes. If you are going to prove how many day people did not show up and the reasons, it won't look good for the picture. I gave to you a very good story and you should be satisfied. I could tell you the reasons why it cost so much money. I admit it is my fault. Two years from now, I will tell you how it happened. Right now, I can't afford it.

SLAVIT: In the current situation, where an artist like Mankiewicz has greater authority probably than any other director has ever had ... this is why it is interesting.

SKOURAS: I cannot afford to tell you certain things. So, I assume all the responsibility of any wrong. I have only one desire – to make the great picture of all times.

SLAVIT: I would not be party to any of this if I did not believe it might be the greatest picture of all time.

SKOURAS: Joe Mankiewicz set the date. I was not there ... I had nothing to do with when the picture started ... it was set at the Studio.

SLAVIT: Re: Brodsky and Weiss, I asked Mr. Zanuck and he did not say it was impossible.

SKOURAS: Joe set the date to start the picture.

SLAVIT: Walter Wanger wanted to postpone it until Spring.

SKOURAS: Wanger wanted to postpone the picture to December, after all the people were on payroll. The picture would cost $10,000,000 more.

Printed in Great Britain
by Amazon.co.uk, Ltd.,
Marston Gate.